Journaling The Journey: 25 Spiritual Insights to Light The Way

by Larry Pearlman

ISBN: 978-1-617-50838-7

Contents

Acknowledgements

The Lone Ranger. That's what I have frequently thought myself to be – especially when it comes to work. Guess that's why I loved my career in sales so much. As long as I was making quota, my boss left me alone. I had nobody reporting to me. I was doing it on my own! Never mind that there were all those people in customer service, operations, engineering, administration, accounting, and the executive staff. Oh…did I mention customers!!?? And then of course there was support from my wife, my son, my friends……………..

Well – writing a book is a lot like that. I saw it as a "personal" thing. My great calling. Time for the Lone Ranger to ride again!! Not even close! So here are just some of the "Tontos" that helped me get this done.

I'd like to start by thanking Mel Brodsky. Bugs – besides being a great friend all of these years, it was when you wrote your first book, *Questions are the Answers*, that I was inspired to write the book that had been in my head only as a floating idea for decades. Guess that shouldn't have been a surprise as "inspiration" is your middle name!

Of course, this would have been simply a travelogue and diary without any Spiritual Insights if it weren't for my spiritual teachers. I specifically owe HUGE posthumous appreciation to Jack and Ruth Pearlman, my parents, for being such excellent examples of spiritual wisdom appearing as kindness, patience, openness, love, and good old common sense. Any conscious understanding of spiritual laws that I was blessed with came as a direct result of the dozen years or so that I was privileged to know Martin Cecil (later Martin Exeter when he assumed his family's English title), both from his own teachings and my exposure, through Martin, to the teachings of Lloyd Arthur Meeker (known as Uranda).

Other spiritual teachers that I had along the way included John and Carol Amey, John and Pam Gray, Bill Bahan, George Emery, Jim Wellemeyer, Michael and Nancy Cecil, Roger DeWinton, Dorothy Hughes (later known as Dorathy Williams), and Alan Hammond.

My close friends Kimberly Amadeo and Phyllis Warren helped me see how my first draft could be improved and then patiently pointed out that the second draft wasn't all that great either! So, if you think this is an enjoyable, inspiring, well-written book, you might send a thank you to Kimberly and Phyllis!

My favorite, and only, but she'd be my favorite even if I had 8, sister Carol was amazing in making sure I had commas where they belong and not where they don't. She also showed me the folly of my ways in starting sentences with "But", although I left a few of those in just because I'm stubborn. I might also mention that there would not be a single "whom" in this book without her guidance. It is amazing to me how much painstaking time Carol put in to help make her little brother look good. I love you, Sis!

David Banner, author of 6 books himself and a kindred spirit, also gave me valuable editorial comment without pulling any punches. It was his comments that saved you from exposure to an appendix that wasn't any more useful than the one in your body. Along with David, Michael Gaetta also took time from his very busy life to give me publishing advice. Rich Kenny turned me in the direction of e-publishing.

Pam Holloway gave me the idea of making the book into an actual journal rather than just using my journal entries. I think that was brilliant. She also helped me think of things to make the book better. Thanks Pam.

It is so much more fun using the actual names of the people in my life, so I would also like to thank the following people for granting me permission to use their real names in this book: John and Carol Amey, Ed Ordower, Joe and Sue Kittel for their son Aaron who has passed on, Carol Winkler, Jean Harvey, Dharma Kellherer, Cliff Penwell, Kate O'Brien, Mel Brodsky, Sharon Pettett, Michael Cecil, Mary (Bane) Pearlman, and Phyllis Warren. I also used actual first names for Debbi, Michael, Rich, Toren, and Jason. All other names mentioned in the writing and in the journal entries have been changed and any resemblance to actual people who might have been present at the times of my life referenced is coincidental.

Preface

You know how you read an inspiring book and think, "WOW – that was awesome! I am going to make some changes that will alter the course of my life," but then somehow you never get around to it? Well – maybe that's never happened to you but, either way, I don't want this to be *that* kind of book. (You're going to hear a lot about what this book is *not* as we go along). So rather than just giving you a peek into my journal and my insights about life, this book is to serve as *your* journal and an opportunity to develop your own life-altering insights. There is a journaling section following each chapter (or feel free to use your own – I won't feel hurt).

After each chapter, there is an opportunity to reflect on the Spiritual Insights presented in that chapter and to journal about your thoughts and feelings related to how those insights apply to your life. I have included some questions as possible starting points, but, hey, what do I know about your life or your way of journaling? You might consider those questions or ignore them and take a whole different direction. You might go to the journaling section of the book after each chapter, after each Spiritual Insight, after you finish the whole book, or after each time you see the word "finagle", which isn't actually anywhere in the book but I like the word so I thought I'd stick it in here. However you choose to include your journaling practice, take your time. This is not the kind of book that is meant to be read in one sitting (See – I told you that you would be hearing a lot about what this book is not.) It is my hope that when you finish the book, you will have had an opportunity for deep reflection and had some personal revelations that may indeed alter the nature of your experience and the course of your life.

There is no such thing as a journaling expert (apologies to those of you who are). By that, I mean that there is no right or wrong way to journal. Each person approaches journaling in the way that will be most creative and useful for him/her. I know that I got tremendous value out of keeping the journal that forms the foundation for the storyline of this book. In fact, that journal, which was so very valuable to me at the time that I was keeping it, proved to be even more valuable later in my life as I reconsidered those thoughts and events.

Journaling is like that. It is a wonderful way to focus your thoughts and feelings in the present moment while at the same time taking snapshots of your experience that may prove useful to whomever you become. Not to mention the pleasure it brings you just thinking of the shocked looks on the faces of some that think they know you well should they read your journal. That might well happen after you die………or when you publish your book. So for those of you who have never journaled before, give it a shot. I think you'll have a creative and joyful experience.

Enjoy the book and enjoy the process.

Introduction

Thirty-seven years ago, when I was 28, I left my good-paying, enjoyable job, family, life-long friends, and the woman every man would love to have as a girlfriend to go on a journey. Didn't know exactly where I was going, how I'd get there, or how long it would take. Didn't make any reservations, had only the loosest of plans, and left with VERY limited funds and whatever belongings I could fit in my 1973 Corvette convertible (cherry red and named Foxy Lady but affectionately known as Fox for those interested in such things). Pointed her nose south and took off.

Sounds exciting, daring, and scary, doesn't it? Well – it was!! And everybody I spoke to about it said something like, "Boy, I wish I could do that" - which convinced me that this trip would make a great book. After all, take any experience that most people will relate to – either based on experience or fantasy – and it should be a best seller. Simple! Well – OK – so it probably has to be interesting, with humor, pathos, adventure, fascinating characters and well written but I figured those were minor points to be dealt with down the road (so to speak). At the time, my intricate plan for this world-wide best-seller was….keep a journal. Yep – that's it. Just write down where I go, whom I meet, where the best burger joints are on the road, my feelings about all that and a bit of insightful observation and BAM – move over Dr. Phil, Wayne Dyer, and Deepak Chopra – there's a new guru in town!

So, I kept a journal. OK – so maybe I wasn't as consistent as I should have been. I might have missed a day here or 6 months there, but I was fairly good about recording my experience for 12 months on the road and sporadically (Well – maybe less than sporadically – is there a word for that?) after I had settled in Phoenix. That yellow notebook sat in my car/suitcase/drawer/garage for 30 years. When I finally decided I didn't want to die with my books (yeah – plural – by this time I'd thought up 2 more brilliant ideas for literary fame and fortune) still in me. I took the next step. I typed the whole journal into WORD so it would be easy to work with. "Easy" is a relative term. Somehow I just never got the motivation/inspiration/flash of genius to get past the title, "The Journey."

Then, 13 days shy of being a 62 year-old Peace Corps Volunteer in my 22nd month in Ghana, it hit me. My journey has been about a lot more than my "Route 66" (if you don't recognize that reference, ask your father….or grandfather) adventure from N.J. to Arizona. It included SO much more up to and including the bucket bath I was enjoying in my cement "bath room" at the time of this bolt from the blue. Maybe that's why the literary muse hadn't lit my flame 'til now – right title but wrong topic.

SPIRITUAL INSIGHT #1: You WILL get Divine inspiration, AND it will manifest according to a Divine timetable – which often will not match the timing you had in mind. Patience truly is a critical step in every creative cycle.

There you have it – the first of 25 spiritual insights that I'd like to share with you within the story that unfolded in my journal. For those who were really looking forward to hearing about the Corvette journey across the U.S., don't fret. It's included. The plan is to look inside the head/heart of the 28/29-year-old Larry Pearlman via journal entries from that trip across the U.S. and insert spiritual insights that the 65-year-old Larry Pearlman has learned since and how they relate to those earlier experiences.

So why should you buy this book? What's in it for you? Well, I'd like to think that you will find it both entertaining and insightful enough that it could lead to significant changes in your life experience. Granted, it won't accomplish both of those things for every person who reads it, but it just might do it for YOU.

So hop in my Corvette, we'll drop the top, turn on the tunes, fire up the CB radio (ask someone born before 1980 about that one) and hit the road.

Chapter 1

Get Thee Out of Thy Father's House

Whoa!! Don't panic! For those of you who are as frightened of a bible reference as a young cowboy on a half-broke horse in front of a rattlers' den, it's just a fitting way to open this chapter. You'll see why soon enough. And just to make sure you don't shut the book (or turn off your Kindle) before the second paragraph, if bible stuff does scare you, skip down to the next paragraph. If that applied to you……… why are you still reading this? You were supposed to skip to the next paragraph. So GO already! For you folks who like bible references and God in particular, this book may not show up in the "Religious" section of your local library, but there will be plenty of God's Word throughout the book. I'm sure you'll recognize it. I didn't hide it all that much.

So …. Let's get this party started.

> Nov 6, 1975 – E. Hanover, N.J. – 9:00 am
>
> The note on the kitchen table said, "Ed, call Lou to set up the Friday night poker game." So…. Life goes on without me. Isn't that amazing – somehow, things will continue as always even though I'm leaving. What is it that Jim Rohn says, "Things will be ….. about like they've always been."

That is the first entry of my journal. You do remember the journal, right? I mean, come on, I just told you about it in the intro, and you're only on page two of Chapter 1. I'll continue just a bit further with my journal entry that day just to put us both in the mental and emotional space of the 28-year-old Larry Pearlman.

> But today starts my Big Adventure. What will I find out as I go forth to meet Life? I hope I find out some things about me.
>
> My mind isn't scared and I've always said that's my 52%. But the 48% that is emotion and gut feel is really scared. My insides churn like butter whenever I allow myself to think about it. Usually – I've always managed to keep myself busy enough so I don't have time to think and feel and cry. That's what this record is all about. Maybe I can get down some feelings on paper over the course of this year. That alone might make the whole thing worthwhile.
>
> My mind tells me that Claudia will be all right. My heart really hopes so. Maybe more on this later. Time to pack the car.

"Whoa!," I can hear you saying, "Who is Claudia?" Well, I don't know who Claudia is today because I haven't seen or heard from her for over 30 years. And I've tried several times. Even now I would love to reconnect with her but that's another story. The 1975 Claudia was the world's perfect girlfriend: funny, smart, sexy (she became a model), independent, beautiful, GREAT legs, and, thanks to her Brazilian upbringing, very attentive to the needs of her man. Wouldn't let me help in the kitchen. Propped my feet up, took off my shoes, and found the right channel for me [*for those born after 1980, YES – we had to walk all the way to the TV to change the channel back then*]. Then she would get me something to drink and go finish making dinner. And this was in the mid-70s when Gloria Steinem ruled and a female friend of mine almost broke my wrist because I dared open a door for her.

So, if you are a sane individual, you might want to know why in the world I would leave this incredible woman. All of my friends wondered that at the time and some of them weren't even sane! Well, I'm afraid I have to admit to being even more bizarre and inexplicable. (I heard somewhere that you have to sprinkle your book with five-syllable words to get published.) If you OCD types are now finished going back to count the syllables in "inexplicable," let's continue.

I didn't leave "just" a woman that any man on the planet would have sworn off sports for a year to be with. I also left a great job, family, friends, and a very comfortable life style. In fact, let's go into those categories in a bit more detail so you can solidify your growing suspicion that I'm a complete idiot.

I worked for General Electric as a sales engineer (why does every company have a fancy name for a salesman?) calling on customers in the NY/NJ area. I loved it, and I was very good at it, consistently over quota and finishing in the top five in the whole country one quarter. I was earning $14,100. Might not sound like much but at that time gas was 53¢/ gallon, stamps were 8¢ and the median price of a new home was $38,900. I had bought a brand new Corvette in 1973 for $5,100. Along with my nice salary, I got a company car, expense account, and great benefits and my job was totally secure. Yet I chose to quit during the most severe recession since WWII. The opening line of the *Economic Report of the President* (Nixon, by the way) said, "The economy is in a severe recession. Unemployment is too high and will rise higher." When I left my cushy job **VOLUNTARILY** in Q4, 1975, unemployment was approaching 9% (hmmm….sounds a lot like 2011, doesn't it?). Does the word "FOOL" come to mind?

But we're not done yet. I had grown up in NJ (Exit 143B for those in the know). Though my parents had recently moved to Florida (it's a law that all Jewish New Yorkers have to move to Florida at age 65), all of my other relatives lived within an hour of me. I was sharing a house with Eddie, my best friend since second grade. Almost every other close friend I had in the world was right there. And I was really enjoying my life. Corvette Club meetings on Tuesdays with exciting events almost every month, bowling on Thursday nights, poker on Friday nights, skiing in the winter, and, being single and frugal (OK – cheap, but not when I really wanted something – like that Corvette), having enough money to do whatever I wanted. Hell – I flew out to San Jose (that's in California – a very long way from NJ. Check your map) for a weekend to surprise some friends out there – even though I wasn't sure they would even BE there! They were, and it was worth the money to see the look on their faces when they opened their door!

Brings us right back to …… "WHAT WAS I THINKING?????" Well, I'm not sure what was bouncing around in my brain at that time; but it really doesn't matter because whatever it was, was simply a rationalization. I'm pretty sure it was a brilliant rationalization but, still, just a rationalization (Since this word has SIX syllables, I figured I'd use it three times and hope to get extra credit with the publishers.) The fact is that my "decision" to leave my wonderful life, pack up my Corvette, and "go west, young man", was not a decision at all. Though I didn't realize it at the time, I was actually following Spirit which was telling me, "Get thee out of thy father's house."

For those not familiar with the phrase, this is what God told Abraham in Genesis (12:1 for those from Missouri). The exact words were, "Now the LORD had said unto Abram, Get thee out of thy country, and from thy kindred, and from thy father's house, unto a land that I will shew thee." Now you might wonder why Abram would be required to leave everything that was dear to him in order to please God. Does God take some kind of pleasure in making things tough on people? Is it really true that to lead a spiritual life we have to suffer? Well – this may cause a number of devout religious people to toss this book in the fire, but I am here to tell you that the answer to that question is a resounding *NO*.

> **SPIRITUAL INSIGHT #2: Life was not meant to be hard. We are born into this world with a natural connection to the Divine Design – the ability to know what is most fitting for us to do, the most fitting place to be, the most fitting people with whom to be. This is the definition of true wisdom. As we maintain this clear connection, we will still meet challenges in life but the burden will be easy and the yoke will be light. As we get educated out of this connection to the Divine Design and stop trusting our inner knowing, life gets hard.**

Now don't get me wrong. I am not saying that people *can't* find their spiritual path via a dark tunnel of suffering. In fact, it happens all the time.

I have read a lot of biographies and was always astounded at how many famous people went through hell in their lives before doing extraordinary things. They were pushed out of those cells of comfort (or some were never in them – they started out in hell) and put in a position where they had to either die (or live like they were dead) or come to the realization that they were something other than the pitiful creature that they saw in the mirror. When you squeeze a wet bar of soap, it either goes up or it goes down. Those who did rise up found their way back to the design that life had laid out for them and went on to greatness.

I would like to bring to your attention one such person that I had the privilege and delight to meet just once, but I am thankful for that one meeting. Aaron Kittel was born with Friedreich's ataxia, a disease that

5

causes progressive damage to the nervous system resulting in symptoms ranging from gait disturbance to speech problems. It can also lead to heart disease and diabetes. He was aware, at an early age, that his body would continually deteriorate; and he would very likely die before he reached 35 years of age. He made it to 33.

At his celebration service (he wouldn't call it anything else), several people spoke about his unwavering ability, even at the very end when he could do nothing for himself and his speech was barely recognizable, to make everyone in his presence feel special and loved. His concern was always for the well being of others around him, and he lived his life with joy and flair. You never knew what color his hair or nails would be, and his love for vibrant color showed up in the tie-dyed shirts that he always wore. Even when he was using a wheelchair, he loved going on white-water rafting trips (he would want me to plug SPLORE here – www.splore.org). Through his "handicap," he had discovered the true meaning of his life. Towards the end, he told his father that if they discovered a cure, he didn't think he would want to take it because his disease had been such a gift to him.

Aaron was special but only because he took full advantage of his circumstance to discover, accept, embrace, and express the truth of himself – his Divine identity – Love. The fact is that ALL of us have that same opportunity. Your private brand of what you can see as hell is your business, but are you really any "worse off" than Aaron was?

There are already shelves full of books helping people out of hell back onto the path to light. For those in that tumultuous boat, one book that could be helpful is Michael Brown's "The Presence Process." My book is not about that. I just wanted to make the point that the road to Heaven doesn't **have to** go through hell; but if yours does, see the gift in your circumstance and follow the road signs to Heaven on Earth.

What was actually happening back then to Abram, and in 1975 to me, was a realization in consciousness that something different was required for the fulfillment of his/my life's work on Earth. As long as a person is comfortable, they have no reason to change anything. They are trapped in a fur-lined prison with a stone ceiling. Funny thing is that the door is not locked. In fact, it's wide open but it's sooooooooo comfortable inside why would someone leave?

But God does not require that you go through hell to get to heaven (just thought I'd repeat that - it's that important). That choice is made by individual human beings. The still, small voice of wisdom is always present with every human being on the planet. That includes the mechanic who charges you for work he didn't do. It includes your uncle Dave who embarrasses the family at every gathering. It includes your priest or rabbi, the fifth grade teacher that held you back, and the kid who took your lunch money every day in third grade. It includes the guy who hits .340 and the guy who rides the bench, the woman who owns the zoo and the guy who cleans up the elephant's cage. But most important, it includes you and me. Well, actually, MOST important for you, it includes you. But you can write your own book. This is my story.

The reason it was critical for me (and Abram) to pack up and go was to change the context in which I was living. As I hope I have made clear, it was quite a nice context and, in respect to worldly vision, a very fulfilling place to live. But that's the point .... it was a worldly context. The voice of Spirit related to true meaning in life, that was only vaguely audible to me at that time, could not be easily nurtured nor developed in that context. Fortunately, I could hear that voice just enough, without being conscious of it, to allow myself to be called out of that context and led towards one in which it was much easier to let the voice of Spirit – MY Spirit really – be in position to be expressed more fully and more consciously. For those familiar with the bible story, you know that Abram changed his name to Abraham after this move. In the bible, a change of name indicates a significant change in the person's consciousness. This is the beginning recognition that the One whose voice is heard and the one hearing it are different aspects of the same Being. More on this in later chapters.

So I got the message that I needed to leave my little paradise. Then, since I did not understand at the time why this was necessary, my mind came up with some tidy little rationalization as to why this was a good idea. In any case, it got me moving.

Question was, "To where?"

<u>Possible Questions to Consider in Your Journal</u>

- Do you see some part of your life circumstance as hellish? If so, why might this circumstance be in your life and what message might it contain for you?
- If there is a hellish circumstance in your life, what can you do to express something positive (Heavenly) into that circumstance *even if nothing else in the circumstance changes*? A great reference here is the story of Joseph in Genesis.
- If your life is comfortable, do you still hear a "still, small voice" telling you that there is something more to life than what you already know? How do you think you might experience that "something more"?

Chapter 2

Where Am I Goin'?

OK – So now that I have left my father's house, where am I goin? (For those not from NY, that means "going"). See – this can be the scary part. In my case, I had packed up the car (as much as you can fit in a Corvette), took care of all of the details of what I was leaving behind, and now it was time to hit the road. But I hadn't really done any planning for the "what comes next" part of this little adventure. Well, not quite true. I did have a plan:

1. Go see the folks in Florida.
2. Go to Atlanta for a while.
3. Be in New Orleans a month before Mardi Gras to get established.
4. Keep going west.
5. Get in some skiing.
6. Stop in different places and stay for a while.
7. End up in the Santa Clara Valley (had spent a year previously in San Jose with GE and loved it).
8. Pay for all this by getting some kind of job every place I stop.

Even with this grand business plan, I couldn't get the bank to finance my venture; so I was pretty much on my own. As you might imagine, on a day-to-day basis, it wasn't the grand adventure it promised to be back when I was packing the car. Consider this journal entry 18 days after leaving NJ:

Nov 24, 1975 – Atlanta – 11:05 pm

Found a place to live today although I don't move in until tomorrow night. $85/month and the place is pretty nice – especially compared to most of the places I've looked at! Private entrance and private bath – refrigerator but no stove – bedroom and living room – parking in the rear – linens and towels supplied – phone available – all utilities paid. Mrs. Cranford – my landlady-lives upstairs with her 25 year old nephew Dan and they both seem like real nice people.

Or this from the following night:

Nov 25 – 10:00 pm

Too tired to really write tonight. Moved into my new place tonight and wrote to Claudia, Greg, Maureen, and the Folks. More letters tomorrow night. Things better start rolling soon or depression may set in. Days aren't bad since I'm busy but the nights of nothing are bad. Got a phone # of a "nice Jewish girl" from an older lady – "Have I got a girl for you!" Think I'll call her soon. That's what desperation looks like!

Believe me, there were many times when I wondered who had dreamed up this whole idea, why I bought into it, and where I was going.

> **SPIRITUAL INSIGHT #3: When you are listening, God will tell you what to do. But often, God will NOT show you the whole plan, just the next step.**

Let me give you an example of how this works. I spent four years at Rutgers · The State University getting a degree in Electrical Engineering. Note, I did not say "earning" a degree. I finished in the half of the class that makes the top half possible and even at that, I KNOW that I did not meet the required cumulative average in my major. Not that I was dumb mind you. I did great in all those other classes – Philosophy, English Lit., Psychology, Marriage and the Family, Logic, and so forth – I just didn't grasp Engineering concepts real well. Mostly what I learned in my four years was how to play bridge (more valuable during the rest of my life than any Engineering course I took) and that I didn't want to be an engineer.

Consequently, when companies sent representatives to conduct interviews to hire people so they could actually go from being poverty-stricken students to being well-respected, tax-paying employees, I didn't bother going to any of those interviews; AND, I really wasn't all that concerned although my brain was telling me obtaining a job would be a good way to feed my habit of eating. Yet this apparently irresponsible behavior wasn't as bone-headed as it sounds. What was actually happening, although I was not conscious of it at the time, was that my mind was releasing control of the situation over to Spirit. And not just any spirit but the Spirit of God. My mind knew that I was not meant to be an engineer, but it had no clue as to what I WAS meant to be. Somehow I knew that I needed to release the mental approach and follow Spirit.........which led me to a telephone pole.

On this particular pole was a notice that two men from the General Electric Co. were giving a talk that night on "Sales Engineering." Even though that sounded like an oxymoron to me, I felt compelled to attend that talk and was, thereby, led into my grand destiny.............SALESMAN!! Turns out that a "sales engineer" is simply a salesman with an engineering degree so that s/he understands the language and can interface with real engineers in order to sell technical products.

"Blindly" following that subconscious intuition to skip most of the interviews and, then, to take a walk one day that happened to go past that telephone pole led me into a 34-year sales career filled with awards, monetary success, tremendous learning opportunities, and helping countless (well, OK – they are probably countable but I don't want to take the time) people and companies; AND all of that was secondary to **simply be doing what I was meant to do**. I never "worked" a day in my life. Never had a "Blue Monday." Never said "Thank God It's Friday." On many occasions, the thought ran through my head, "They're PAYING me for this!" Even said it out loud a few times. Fortunately, nobody associated with a Behavioral Health Center was within earshot during those times.

My point here is not to try and sell you on Sales as a career path. In fact, I don't know too many people who would enjoy it, and I know several people who would rather chew on aluminum foil. The point is that there is ***something*** that is right for every person. Whatever that something is for you will be something that doesn't feel like work - like when you are in that art class, working on your car, spending hours in the batting cage, cooking, volunteering at a retirement home, gardening, working with horses, or fixing the plumbing. If you haven't found whatever that is for you....................**DON'T GO LOOKING FOR IT!!!** It will find you if you relax, stop turning the crank of your conscious mind, and follow your intuition.

No telling what form that might take. A feeling to drive home by a different route takes you past a sign advertising a free introductory dance class. Talking to the guy who accidentally dented your car reveals the fact that he's looking for someone to help on his ranch, and he's willing to train you. Applying to the Peace Corps (we'll get to that part of my life later) turns into a chance encounter with someone in a charitable organization looking for someone to work with children in third world countries. In other words, your mind (wonderful as it is) simply cannot plan the route that will lead you to your telephone pole. Face it – as much as you know (and I'm sure you're a very smart person or you wouldn't have bought my book), it can't be even .01% of everything; but your intuition is connected to the other 99.99% so let it work for you.

Oh – one more point about following your intuition. Remember Spiritual Insight #3? Go ahead – back up a couple of pages and refresh your memory. I'll wait here.

Good – you're back. So – not only doesn't God reveal the whole plan ahead of time, you may or may not get recognizable confirmation of the accuracy of your decisions. Sometimes you do. Like when I was 16 years old and on the way home from Jean's house (she was my first love back in high school). I had carried her books home from school (yes – we really did that in those days. Your grandfather wasn't making it up) and was now crossing the foot bridge over the railroad tracks headed home. I saw a huge train coming and decided to watch it pass under me. For those who have never stood on a bridge watching a train pass, it is so cool! Then I remembered that I had left something at Jean's house. I wanted to wait until after the train passed to go get it but followed a feeling to go back for it NOW. When I returned to that foot bridge, it was laying in a crumpled heap far below on top of the train which had jumped the track and taken out the supports of the bridge. Somewhere in the midst of that wreckage would have been my broken and lifeless body had I not listened to that inner voice. I wasn't conscious of it at the time but that may have been the first significant time I actually followed Spirit.

That was one of the rare times that it was immediately obvious that I had made the right choice. Most of the time, you don't get that feedback. You feel like you should take a different route home from work and keep waiting to see *why* that feeling came up. Nothing, however, unusual happens. Well, maybe there was an accident waiting to happen on the other route. Perhaps you simply needed to be a few minutes later getting home for some reason (see the movie, "Sliding Doors"). The fact is that we don't see the "why", the revelation of the Divine Design, very often. So how do we know when we make the fitting choice, the wise decision? Oh, come on. You know the answer to that. When you're honest with yourself AND you take the time to relax and release your turbulent thoughts and emotions, you ALWAYS know in your gut whether what you did was right or not.

Like right now – I just know that this is the place to end this chapter. You may feel like I'm cheating you because I still haven't told you where I was going on this journey; therefore, you may not be happy about this decision.

SPIRITUAL INSIGHT #4: It's not my job to make you happy, nor is it your job to make anyone else happy. Your job is to be true to the Truth of yourself; and if you pay attention, you will always know what that is. Good news: it usually involves joy.

<u>Possible Questions to Consider in Your Journal</u>

- Have you ever had a gut feeling to do something that seemed to make no sense but you followed it anyway? How did it work out?
- Are you the type of person who needs to know (or think you know) exactly how things are going to go before you will take the first step? Does it always work out the way you thought it would? Would you have started down that path if you knew how it was *actually* going to work out? What does this say about your trust in Life?
- How much of what you do is done to make someone else happy? Does it work out well for both of you? Think of a situation that is current for you where you KNOW what you should do but you are hesitating or even going in a different direction because you think it will make someone else happy. Visualize doing what you know is right and see how it makes you feel.

_____
_____
_____
_____
_____
_____
_____
_____
_____
_____
_____
_____
_____
_____
_____
_____
_____
_____
_____
_____
_____
_____
_____
_____
_____
_____

Chapter 3

Do You Know The Way to San Jose?

That was my destination – San Jose. I didn't know much about how this trip was going to go, how long it would take, what would happen along the way, or what I would do when I got there, but I was darn sure of one thing – **I was going to end up in San Jose or somewhere in the Santa Clara Valley!**

Actually………….. that never happened.

But at least it gave me a feeling that I wasn't **totally** without direction. That's a useful thing. It gives the mind something to hold on to while Spirit is having its way directing you. And Spirit always does a pretty good Job. Consider this entry on my first day in New Orleans.

<u>Jan 10, 1976 – Sat – 10:30 pm – New Orleans</u>

Far out!! [*People talked like that in the 70s*] This morning I was in Atlanta with my friends and tonight it starts over again. New city – no friends – HELL, not even any <u>acquaintances</u>!! No job – no address – no phone. Life is really amazing. Two months from now when I'm ready to start all over again, I will have built a foundation of a life in New Orleans: friends, a job, a place to live, a familiarity with the area – and as soon as that feeling of comfort and security begins to drape itself over me – out comes Barry's sign: "Escape – While There's Still Time"!!

If you're wondering who Barry is, I'm not really sure; but I think it was a guy I worked with in NJ. Anyway, his sign may have been Spirit's way of telling me to be very careful not to re-create "my father's house" all over again. It's amazing how often people do that (not you or me of course!). They get it that they need to get out of their situation (relationship – job – neighborhood – family dynamics – whatever) and summon up the courage to do just that. Then they sink right back into the same morass without noticing because things look different on the outside so we think something has actually changed. What's wrong with this picture?? Simple:

SPIRITUAL INSIGHT #5: Until you recognize the ways in which YOU need to change and then actually make those changes, your external circumstances, no matter how different they look, will never alter your internal experience.

Let me give you an example out of my life that I'm guessing is pretty common. Who knows – it might even apply to you. I found that in relationships, whether girlfriend, wife, (those two did not exist simultaneously!), son, friend, boss, etc, there would come a time when I would have a disagreement with the other person. In those instances where I KNEW I was right, and the other person was just being stubborn, those conversations rarely went well – primarily because they knew THEY were right, and I was just being stubborn! If it was a recurring situation, then I could have recorded our conversation the first time it came up and just played it back each subsequent time. In fact, doing that would have saved us both a lot of heartache as we could have left the room and gone out for coffee and Danish while the argument was going on!

Finally, one day, a light came on. I was in a motel room with a wonderful woman that I loved. We were on vacation in Flagstaff, Arizona (Hey – it might not be Kauai, but Flagstaff has beautiful mountains and forests. Visit some time. You'll like it.). We were getting ready for bed when something (do we ever really remember what starts arguments?) went awry, and we began the usual downward spiral. At about the 70% escalation point, where loving, cuddling, and sex were definitely out of the picture, I stopped. I looked at her, took a deep breath, let my anger go and gently and lovingly said, "We both know exactly where this is headed. We've been there before. I really don't want to go there tonight. Do you?" The impending disaster was averted and all the lovey-dovey stuff that had gone out the window came back in the door and we shared a beautiful night together.

Made me wonder why all the arguments before, with her and others before her, needed to happen at all. The external circumstances – people involved, cause of argument, type of relationship, etc – had kept changing and none of that made any difference. When something changed *in me* and I was willing to release my need to be right in favor of honoring and cherishing the relationship, THEN a different outcome was possible.

The fact is that you (I, they, we, whoever - Might as well get this out in the open now for all of you English teachers. I plan to mix my pronouns unmercifully in this book. Just too tedious to make sure I'm consistent. So sue me.) never REALLY had to make those external changes at all. The only reason that we are led to do so is that Spirit hopes that the change of scenery will enable us to refocus our attention on what really DOES need to change – the internal landscape, the understanding of true identity, who I really am. That is the most important question in your life – who are you REALLY? That's the biggie – the Grand Poobah of all questions – so I can't answer that for you yet. Too early in the book. How much could I charge for a book if it only had three chapters?? We'll get to that later.

Based on the title of this chapter, you may have thought we were going to talk about San Jose. In fact, when you started this book, some of you may have hoped for some fascinating insights into the places I was travelling through – so far, Atlanta and New Orleans. Well – I have good news and bad news. The good news is that I did take notes on interesting things in each city I visited, and I had summarized that incredibly enlightening information in an appendix to this book. The bad news is that it is information from the 1970s, so it's about as useful as a street map to Atlantis. Upon reading it myself, after a good friend questioned why on earth I thought ANYONE would want to read it, I deleted my beloved Appendix. I mean, how many people actually read the *Appendix* in ANY book?? The fact that they call it the "appendix" should tell you something about how useful it is!!

But I digress. (By now, that's not a big surprise to you.) Let's get back to the question of how I got from knowing nobody in New Orleans to having a place to live, a job, a girlfriend (Joan – had some great times together but that's another book. Be sure to write to the publisher and demand that they publish more of my stuff), a bank account, and all of the stuff that makes up a life. Sure, I could say that it was a lot of phone calls (no internet back then), answering ads, and talking to people; but why did I make THOSE calls, answer THOSE ads, and talk to THOSE people? Why did I stop at the Travel-Lodge when I first reached New Orleans instead of the Ramada? Why did the General Manager (who just happened to have been in a similar situation to mine 30 years before) happen to be walking through the lobby when I was telling the desk manager that I needed to talk to the General Manager about getting a job there instead of leaving a resume? Why did I walk into the 5-7-9 Shop that Joan managed when I had zero need for anything they sell? Why am I asking all of these questions?

There are three ways that these things happen.

1. Through your own self will, you create an iron-clad plan, or accept someone else's (read "parents", "society", "spouse", etc) and then MAKE it happen. My experience is that this can, in fact, work. It is, however, generally exhausting, ultimately unfulfilling, and often leaves a swath of dead and injured in its path. The negative impact of this approach can be lessened if it is blended with some mixture of the following two approaches.
2. While bumbling along in life or bulling your way through the china shop with approach #1, God keeps putting road signs in front of you. Consider this entry while on a flight to Aspen from New Orleans:

<u>3/8/76 - Monday – 1:15 pm – In Flight</u>

Made a short stop in Houston and am now on the way to Denver. Fell asleep for a while and when I woke up there was a girl sitting next to me reading a book about Revelation. Seems like Stuart Schipman was right. The Lord keeps putting people in my path. She is a Christian in the same sense that he is and we have been talking for the last hour. I don't think I'll be able to stay apart from this subject. Eventually I will have to face it and make a decision.

Y'think??!! For a while, the signs tend to be gentle and even subtle like a nice person sitting next to you on a plane reading a book about Revelation. If you continue to ignore them or even rebel against them, however, you may very well end up getting hit with a 2 x 4 that still has 6-penny nails in it. (Is that a big nail? I'm not much of a carpenter!) Could be ill health, recurring bad relationships, a string of "accidents", financial "disaster", or any one of a number of things designed to get the attention of someone who hasn't been listening. Approach #2 only works if you FINALLY get the message before driving off the cliff.

3. Actually listening: Opening one's senses to hear that "still, small voice" within. I gave you two examples of that from my life in Chapter 2. Oh come on – that was just in the last chapter, and it was dramatic stuff – one time it saved my life, and one time it decided my life's career path. Well, maybe it wasn't as important to you as it was to me, but I'm hoping that you at least remember reading about it. You might also remember Spiritual Insight # 1 – "Life is not meant to be hard." That's what Option 3 is all about. If we just pay attention to our instinct, our intuition, our hunches, we discover that we don't have to attend the School of Hard Knocks for decades in an attempt to figure out all of the things that DON'T work in order to see what does.

I know what you're thinking – I mean besides how attractive your new co-worker is. You're remembering all those times when you did follow your instinct, and it didn't work out all that well. Perhaps cutting across the farmer's field where the bull grazes didn't qualify you for Einstein-of-the-Year Award. So let's take a moment to talk about those other voices in your head that often masquerade as Spirit.

There are dozens of them, and that's conservative. Some belong to your mother, your father, the fifth-grade bully, the ex-girlfriend that said you'll never amount to anything, the teacher that taught you to only color between the lines, the religious leader that taught you that God and miracles are WAY beyond you, and ....well, you fill in the ones that take up the most space in YOUR head. I, however, want to key in on just two – although these are most likely influenced by, or composites of, the others. One is the voice of your emotions and the other is the voice of reason.

The voice of your emotions is actually one voice, but it comes in many flavors - fear, lust, joy, anger, grief, passion, and angst just to name a few. This is often the loudest voice in the crowd and the easiest to follow. There are few guarantees in life but it's a good bet that if you make a habit of following this voice, you are going to be putting out fires more often than the NYFD during a pyromaniac's convention.

The fact that this is the easiest voice to follow is the reason that so few people find their way to their naturally-flowing place within the Divine Design without wending their way through a whole bunch of pot-hole ridden, life-shattering detours. I'm not suggesting that there is anything wrong with emotions. They are a vital part of whom we are and play a huge role in being human. But they are not in place to run the show. More on this in Chapter 5.

The voice of reason takes a shot at trying to convince you that your *mind* is supposed to be in charge. After all, look how much trouble you get in when you're pulled around by the nose (or, for men, too often by some other part of your anatomy) by those pesky emotions. Surely you can see that it will be far better for you to listen to the sane, rational, reasonable inhabitant of the left half of that duplex we call a brain. Stay in that place and you will likely live an ordered, less risky, predictable, but boring existence. On occasion, you may even have a near-life experience! As important as the rational mind is (try living without it!), it is also the place of limitations. It is the place of definitions based on observable facts.

SPIRITUAL INSIGHT #6: There will ALWAYS be infinitely more that you DON'T know than what you DO know – about EVERY situation.

Accepting this as true, we can then see how it is totally UNREASONABLE to make decisions based solely on the information contained in the conscious, rational mind. If you don't believe that Spiritual Insight #6 applies to you, just think about all those times when you were absolutely sure of something and then discovered that it was not true. If you're having trouble coming up with any, ask your spouse, parent, or child. They'll be glad to help.

So if we can't count on either emotions or reason to lead us down the path that is truly right and creative for us, than what voice DO we listen to? Good question and you already know the answer. That's

THE point of this chapter and one of the main points of this book. To find the road less traveled – the road paved with fulfillment, creativity, love, and joy in living – we listen to the voice of Spirit– the voice we hear when we still the mind and the heart so that they are ready to follow rather than trying to lead. It's not a question of eliminating your mind and your emotions – that's commonly called death. The fact is that, as powerful as Spirit is, it cannot manifest on this planet except THROUGH the mental and emotional realm combined with the physical. That is **why** emotions and reason are vital parts of whom we are. I mean, did you really think that God gave you a brain and a heart just to befuddle you?

Let's go back to examples. They are much easier to understand. Besides, if you can't come up with an example of something then how valid could it really be? I have already said that it was Spirit that truly led me to embark on this journey from NJ to San Jose. But you can't just tell your friends and family that God is calling you to quit your job and head off on some amorphous trip that has no apparent purpose. Well, you COULD do that but then there would be a messy intervention and possibly a short stay as a guest of a state-run institution where they don't let you keep your belt.

Actually, at that point in my life, I couldn't even tell **myself** that! So Spirit takes that seed and plants it in the subconscious mind as an idea. The conscious mind would probably reject it as a harebrained, half-cocked, screwy idea. So Spirit also works through the emotions which told me that this would be an exciting, educational, perhaps life-changing journey. This is appealing enough to the mind that it begins to rationalize how this is the perfect time to take such a risk and I can always just come back if it doesn't work out.

And THAT, my friends, is how you find the way to San Jose. Unless, of course, you're not supposed to end up there. I feel another song title coming on.

Possible Questions to Consider in Your Journal

- Has there been a pattern in your life with relationships, jobs/bosses, places where you live/neighbors, or something else where the external circumstances (your lover, job, neighborhood, etc) have changed, perhaps several times, yet the same challenges keep arising? What might you do to change your experience of this pattern given that the people and other externals involved are NOT going to change?

- Think of a time in your life where you forged ahead in the strength of your will to accomplish something, ignoring that still small voice inside that was telling you it was not the right direction. How did it turn out? How much of your energy did it take, even if you were "successful"? In the long run, did it bring you fulfillment? Now think of a time when you followed your intuition to move in a direction that you didn't want to go or didn't understand. How did THAT turn out? Did it drain you or energize you? Did it lead to greater fulfillment?

- Can you think of any "signposts", Divine hints, or intuitive feelings that have been coming up for you in recent days? What would it take to act on them?

- What internal "voices" do you hear? Which have proved to be creative in your life? How do you differentiate among the voices of emotion, in all of its guises, cold reason, and Spirit? How does Spirit act through your emotions and your conscious mind?

Chapter 4

Love is a Many Splendored Thing

When I arrived in Houston, I wondered out loud how it compared to Dallas, where I had never been. I was told by a big, brash Texan (is there any other kind?), "Son, Houston is where people MAKE money. Dallas is where people SPEND money." This, of course, got me thinking about money. Seems like everybody is always concerned about it. Consider this partial entry from New Orleans:

<u>Feb 3 – Tuesday – 8:30 pm</u>

I finally got my load of mail in from Gerry and among the normal bad news – Shell and Amoco are past due, Mike missed a payment, and my old savings account shows I closed out with a $21 deficit – came this little jewel – Arizona Title & Insurance claims I owe them $800 for the balance of my account on my Lake Havasu land!! Needless to say – I'll get them off a letter tomorrow.

Money is for sure going to be a BIG hassle when I hit Houston. I'll have about $310 plus $100 in matured bonds but I can't expect to see any kind of a paycheck right away and will have to make my $162 car payment [*TIME WARP: $162/mo for a CORVETTE!!!*] plus my car insurance payment ($180) will be due then, I'll have to pay <u>somebody</u> rent and maybe a security deposit as well, I owe B/A over $600 on paper and over $400 of that will be on the bill Gerry has now, and who knows what other bills will come up. Plus – the Unemployment people say I'm only eligible for $90 – I hope they send <u>that</u> fast! Of course, Miriam still owes me $100 from my commodities account, Maureen owes me $64 and Mike owes me $269 but I can't count on the cavalry coming on time. If I have to, I'll cash some US bonds a bit prematurely.

Actually, I probably could have let my journal fall open, and there would have been some entry dealing with money (probably right next to one dealing with sex). It may have started earlier in my life but the first time I can remember thinking about how broke I was, was when I was a freshman in college and had to look for someone to bum 6 cents from to buy a stamp (remember those days?!). While floundering in my pity pool at the time, I realized that I was in college with my tuition, books, room, and 21 meals/week paid for. I had all the clothes I needed. I was able to work and part time jobs were available. Maybe I didn't have any "extra money" (whatever that is) but I was probably in a better financial condition than a good percentage of the world's population.

Then I started to notice that just about everybody thinks they have less money than they "need." The person living on the street needs a roof. The person in an apartment needs a house. The person with a bike wants a car. The person with ..... Well – you get the idea. It never seems to end. The person with a million dollars in the bank STILL doesn't feel secure!

Wanna' know why?

OK – By now you are wondering if you are in the wrong chapter. You're saying to yourself, what the heck is he talking about and what does this have to do with love? Well – here it comes. Let's start with that last question again.

Wanna' know why?

It's because money is just a substitute for something far more precious – love. Ever know a couple who scrimped and scratched and sacrificed through hard times together and then split up when things got "better"? Maybe you were one of those people. If you are expressing love in your life but have no money (kinda' sounds like Jesus, Mohammed, Gandhi, Mother Theresa, Buddha....doesn't it?), you always have enough. If, however, you have enough money to fill Ft. Knox and don't express love in your life.........you're broke and you can never get enough money to change that.

I'm not suggesting that you burn all your money and then you will know true peace and fulfillment. If you really find it a burden, though, I am now spiritually advanced enough that you can send it all to me, and I'll handle it rightly! Money is not the point. Live a life of love, and you will be fulfilled with or without money. Hell – you might be rolling in it or not have a dollar in your pocket. MONEY IS NOT THE POINT!!

SPIRITUAL INSIGHT # 7: Man does not live by bread alone.

OK – I know that one did not originate with me, but it just goes to show how long this truth – ALL truth for that matter – has been around. The rest of that thought had to do with the Word of God. Well – that word is LOVE.

I know I mentioned the young, struggling but loving couple before, and that really is a good example of what we are talking about; but I'm not just talking about romantic love between two people, although I certainly have given that some thought. For instance, here is my journal entry from Feb 4, 1976:

Feb 4 – Wed – 7:30 pm

What is "being in love"? Maybe everyone has their own definition that fits them. When I am "in love" – and I hope that someday I will be – I want to think about that person all of the time – and feel good and warm inside every time I do think of her. I want to miss her whenever I go away – even if I'm gone only a day or two. And it must be her that I miss – not just a warm body or pleasing personality that usually keeps me company or shares my bed at night. I don't want just someone who I'm 'used to' and get along with well. That's not what I think love should be. Am I wrong? Am I waiting for something that doesn't even exist? I don't believe that. I can't believe that. It's no ego trip that I'm on that tells me Claudia is in love with me – she has found what I am yearning for only I cannot respond to it because I DON'T LOVE HER the same way! When I do find that feeling, I pray that it is a two-way love. What agony to find something so incredibly precious only to have it be incomplete because it only goes one way.

Am I being too cautious? Paranoid? I don't think so. How many people make the mistake of prolonging a relationship merely because it's comfortable – and often not even that! It's just easier to stay with the status quo. At this point, it seems senseless to commit more months and years of my life and her life to the cause of a comfortable relationship. Perhaps if I get to be 50 and still haven't found what I seek – then it will be time to change the goal and merely seek out a companion.

And here's an entry from a looooong time later in my life, when I was closing in on 50, with a bit different perspective. I could have just given you the "love" part but thought you might find the rest interesting. I did!!

<u>January 26, 1993 – Tuesday – 11:26 PM</u>

Welcome to Pearlman's Journal – Volume II. The last entry in Volume I was made over 15 years ago. One third of my life has passed since then. That third will just have to go unrecorded. What the hell – I only recorded memories of 1 year of the 30 preceding that! Time to move on.

Why am I back, you ask? Compulsion. Time to get back in touch. Time to read more and maintain my journal. Time for creativity and sharing. Time for the heart to step more to the fore. Even wrote a poem the other day. First time in a long time. Writer's block is a bit scary when all you are writing is your thoughts. No thoughts!! Maybe I'm just out of practice. There's a good reason to start this again. Cancel the T.V., telephone, food, work, all the distractions and really be present with Me and see what's here. If I am to have something to offer that is genuine, I have to get in touch with it before I can really share it.

Love comes to mind. What is it <u>really?</u> I've never discovered the romantic love sought after by many and claimed by few. Is that real or myth? My conviction is that Love is unconditional. That's not an adjective defining a type of love. That's an inherent characteristic of Love. If it's Love, it is unconditional. If it isn't unconditional, it isn't Love. Love is not directional. I don't Love something or somebody. I just Love. It could be called omni-radiant. Love exudes from me and goes out like an enlarging sphere – not like a laser. Again – that is a characteristic of Love – inherent. Until I Love all, I don't truly know Love – just perhaps an inkling of it. Does that mean I stop smashing roaches or do I know them in Love and smash them anyway? Not sure yet. I'll get back to you on that.

That's what I'm talking about now - the all-encompassing, omni-directional love of life exhibited by Jesus, Gandhi, and others who truly understood. The kind of love that does not judge, condemn, blame, or criticize but rather uplifts, supports, enhances, and appreciates all life.

Here are some ways it might look as recorded in my earlier journal:

<u>February 1, 1977 – Tuesday 8:30 PM</u>

I just had an adventure – I went to the library!! Adventure? You bet – a glorious, much-too-short (fleeting even), adventure in Life. I wish I could bottle it – or even just be able to summon it at will. Description fails me. I just felt free and alive and giving – like I was bringing Life and spark to whomever I talked to. It was a break from my norm and it returned me to that super light state that I feel so natural in. I Love it. I <u>knew</u> there was more to living than television and sleeping!!

<u>February 27 – Sunday – 8:00 AM</u>

Met an 8 year old boy named Craig on Friday. Craig was in town with his mother to visit various doctors and hospitals to get prepared for upcoming surgery. Craig has no nose. As he left Children's Hospital, he thought of the fact that the hospital had supplied free lunch and a snack around 10:30 and he said to his mother, "Boy Mom – we sure are lucky!" I think I learned something about [loving] Life from Craig.

That's not to say that love is totally amorphous - to the contrary. When you love ALL, you love EACH, and love is expressed in individual ways. The love you have for a puppy, your significant other, the grocery store clerk, the night sky, and a great pitching wedge is (are? – any English majors out there?) not all the same. You feel it and express it in different ways, but the source is the same. True love ALWAYS comes from the Divine – the aspect of you that is a true revelation of God. Let's explore other faces of love.

<u>March 8 – Monday – 1:15 pm - in the air en route to Aspen</u>

Left Fox with Joan, and I'm sure she'll enjoy it. Hope she decides to give her back to me!! I may be stupid for doing things like that and maybe it's irresponsible but I do get a lot of joy and satisfaction out of sharing and watching other people being happy. If I get burned some day, so be it. In the meantime, I prefer to believe that what you put out eventually comes back to you tenfold. I miss Joan but I can't be sure how much of it is due to the loneliness of being alone again. I know she tried to keep away from "making love" so as not to further screw up her head, but there definitely were times that we touched each other – more out of bed than in. Those times were really nice. I hope I just don't mess up her mind again. I really would like to help her get straight again. It's just that I don't know how to get to know someone without reaching in and touching them. Our relationship has been short by time standards, Joan, and mostly sweet – probably 98% sweet. I just hope that it does you more good than harm.

Caring about someone and wanting the best for them is one indicator that love is moving through you. It can be expressed as simply as helping a child who has fallen, smiling at someone passing you on the street, enjoying the look or smell of a neighbor's flower garden, or being on time when you are meeting someone who values punctuality. Sure, there are bigger ways of showing love. Maybe you went to Louisiana or Mississippi after Hurricane Katrina. Maybe you adopted a handicapped child. Maybe you donated a large sum of money to a charity that touches your heart. However you offer it, it is the same currency.

Yet loving someone and caring deeply for them does not mean that you can always help them along their life path. If they are caught in a destructive pattern – drugs, alcohol, deceit, or any of a thousand other deadly pursuits – and refuse to even consider breaking away from that pattern, there may be nothing you can do to help them. This is painful to watch when it is happening to someone you love – especially when there is little you can do about it if they refuse to change their path.

> **SPIRITUAL INSIGHT # 8: If someone you love is sinking in quicksand and refuses to take the branch you offer but rather insists that you jump in and push them out, your only choices are to sink with them or watch them go under. Choice #1 is always a bad idea!**

While maintaining the integrity of your own life, you continue to offer that person your love even if it appears to be "tough love." In this way, you continue to offer the branch. They must make the choice to grasp it so that you can help them find a way to lead a creative life.

This situation does not only present itself in life experiences where the outcome is obviously life changing. Even seemingly minor choices WILL change the direction of your life. An example. When I was a young, aspiring salesman with General Electric, just before my journey west, I worked in an office with several other people. One man, whom I will call Bertrand just because it's not often I get to use the name Bertrand, used to enjoy complaining a lot. Might be about the crabgrass, our boss, the economy, his car, whatever. If you know anyone like Bertrand, you are familiar with how easy it is to get sucked right into that flavor of quicksand (Note to self: don't use "flavor" and "quicksand" in the same sentence without expecting to gag). Pretty soon, you find yourself saying, "That's nothing. Listen to what happened to ME yesterday." If you've ever been caught in that downward spiral, you might be aware of how bad it feels to your body to go there. Blood pressure up, headache coming on, and, when it's all over, energy drained. So one day I decided to quit jumping into the quicksand. I gently told Bertrand that I would like to hear about the good things that were going on in his life, but I was no longer interested in anything he had a complaint about. I'd love to tell you that Bertrand immediately lit up, shook my hand, and thanked me for having saved him from going straight to hell; but, as you might imagine, the reaction was more like him telling ME to go straight to hell! OK – maybe not that bad, but he chose not to talk to me much for some time after that, which was not all bad for me! Eventually, he did start talking with me again, and I noticed that he saved his complaining for conversations with others. Sad fact is, I didn't change Bertrand's behavior, but I didn't go under with him either. There are lots of ways to ruin your experience of Life other than drugs, booze, and robbing banks. Watch out for the choices you make in the "little things". Those are the things that make up the fabric of your life and give you the daily opportunities to express Love.

The place of love is so expansive that one who is expressing it always finds new relationships with love. This was stated beautifully by Lloyd Arthur Meeker, also known as Uranda:

"Yet, in love there is nothing static, and that which is the revelation of one phase of love is never a complete portrayal of it. We find that no matter how much we may know or have experienced with respect to love, it is only in part, because God's Love is eternal. God's eternal Love is ever issuing forth, and its manifestations are with respect to different conditions, different situations, different focalizations of vibratory factors. So, in detail at least, no experience in any given moment with respect to love is like any other."

So we have looked at just a few of the infinite ways that love expresses itself. And here's a news flash, Bubala – when that is happening through you, YOU ARE LOVE!!

SPIRITUAL INSIGHT # 9: When you know Divine love within, you always have more than enough.

A person's experience with money is a reflection of their love of life. Those who think they live in a hostile universe where you'd better watch your back (hard to do without a mirror!) and always look out for #1 reflect that attitude in a scarcity consciousness. They feel that they can never have enough to really protect themselves. That kind of person is always wondering why things keep coming up requiring their resources so that they can never "get ahead".

Those who see the universe as a loving supportive environment, and know that if you cast your bread upon the waters it will come back buttered and jellied, reflect that attitude in an abundance consciousness. That kind of person is in awe that whenever anything comes up there always seems to be money available somehow to handle it.

As an Emissary Server (see Chapter 8) for many years, I was enabled to perform marriages. I think it is fitting to end this chapter with one of my favorite Bible passages, Corinthians I: 13:1 – 13:13

13:1 Though I speak with the tongues of men and of angels, and have not love, I am become as sounding brass, or a tinkling cymbal.

13:2 And though I have the gift of prophecy, and understand all mysteries, and all knowledge; and though I have all faith, so that I could remove mountains, and have not love, I am nothing.

13:3 And though I bestow all my goods to feed the poor, and though I give my body to be burned, and have not love, it profiteth me nothing.

13:4 Love suffereth long, and is kind; love envieth not; love vaunteth not itself, is not puffed up,

13:5 Doth not behave itself unseemly, seeketh not her own, is not easily provoked, thinketh no evil;

13:6 Rejoiceth not in iniquity, but rejoiceth in the truth.

13:7 Beareth all things, believeth all things, hopeth all things, endureth all things.

13:8 Love never faileth: but whether there be prophecies, they shall fail; whether there be tongues, they shall cease; whether there be knowledge, it shall vanish away.

13:9 For we know in part, and we prophesy in part.

13:10 But when that which is perfect is come, then that which is in part shall be done away.

13:11 When I was a child, I spake as a child, I understood as a child, I thought as a child: but when I became a man, I put away childish things.

13:12 For now we see through a glass, darkly; but then face to face: now I know in part; but then shall I know even as also I am known.

13:13 And now abideth faith, hope, love, these three; but the greatest of these is love.

So, one last insight to conclude this chapter:

SPIRITUAL INSIGHT # 10: The secret to knowing and expressing God is to let Love radiate ***without concern for results.**

Possible Questions to Consider in Your Journal

- Write out 5 ways that you expressed love in your life today. If you have a hard time coming up with them, then make it 5 in the past week or maybe just 2 today. Make it easy on yourself. THAT is an act of love!

- Reflect on your own attitude towards money. Do you have enough? If you believe you need more, forget about finding more money. For the next month, find ways that you can express more love in your life. Begin now by writing down some ways you might do that. At the end of the month, journal about how you then feel about your financial situation.

- What do you find most valuable in your life – people, experiences, activities? How do you feel when you are with those people or doing those things? Is it more valuable to you than money? Are there ways you could increase the time you spend in those situations?

- What are some appropriate ways that you can express the Love that you are to those closest to you? To your co-workers and boss? To your neighbors? To the grocery store clerk and waitress? To someone you don't like very much?

- Do you know anyone sinking in quicksand? How can you reach out to them without jumping in after them?

Chapter 5

Those Pesky Emotions

Way back in chapter 3, I promised that we would talk about emotions - how they can derail our lives and how they can be one of our greatest gifts. Let's look first at how we can be controlled by our emotions and our emotions can be controlled by external events. Consider these two entries from Houston.

<u>June 10 – Thursday – 12:30 PM</u>

Things are picking up – socially and sexually. [*A real juicy part followed this but I already told you I'm not going there in this book so you'll just have to make up your own. I'm skipping to the social scene*] ….. [Cindy]'s getting her own apartment when Flora and her husband get back and I'll have to get her phone #.

I also got Lisa's phone # although – get this – I won't have the <u>time</u> to see her this week! Tonight I'm going to a Charlie Chaplin movie at the JCC. Tomorrow night I'm going out to dinner with Gerry and Sat we're going to Sea-Arama in Galveston. I hope we get along well since we'll be spending all day together!!

Everything's goin' my way, right? Here's the entry from 3 days later.

<u>June 13 – Sunday – 5:30</u>

The weekend turned out to be a social disaster. The "movie night" at J.C.C. was terrible and there weren't any eligible chicks there – in fact, only about 8-10 people showed up all together!! I only stayed about 20 minutes. Then my Fri and Sat dates with Gerry fell through when her cousin and 3 friends dropped in unexpectedly for the weekend. I did take Cindy to the Drive-In Fri night to see Embryo – which wasn't a bad flick – but 5 minutes after we got home (2:30 AM) her boss called and wanted her to come right over. Naturally, she went. I hope he got plenty because all I got was eaten by 1600 mosquitoes at the movie!! Then I called Lisa and tried to make a date to go to Sea-Arama on Sunday. She told me to call at 9:30 AM on Sunday which I did – she wasn't home!! Nice, huh? Therefore – I went to the autocross [car race]– which I did lousy in!! Not one of my finer weekends.

Well – THAT took a nasty turn!! But it didn't HAVE to make a big difference in my experience.

SPIRITUAL INSIGHT # 11: What *happens* to me does not determine my experience – "good" or "bad". It is how I respond and *what I respond to* that determines my experience. I can choose to respond to the event or I can choose to respond to God – Life – my Higher Power – my True Self. When I do the latter, I am not pulled pillar to post by my emotions.

Let's take a look at what this might look like in real life. All we have to do is check out an entry from less than a week later.

<u>June 19 – Sat – 1:00 AM</u>

Some of my feelings towards Joan are really strange. I called her last Sat and Alberta told me she had gone to Florida for the weekend. Whenever I hear stuff like that – it bothers me. I get kind of mad at her (totally irrational as Mr. Spock would say) and also feel a little hurt. Then she called me a couple days later and we discussed her trip. She went with this guy that she has recently started seeing and naturally they got it on. I knew she wanted to talk with me about it but at the same time she didn't. It's obviously a queer situation! Anyhow, I directed the conversation to the point where we did discuss it and at that time felt none of the above feelings. I just felt affection for her and a real interest in helping her sort out her feelings and thoughts. It was really strange. Of course, she was experiencing some guilt feelings and I don't want that at all. I'll have to help her overcome that if she's going to straighten out her head about her sex life.

This is a great example of how this process can work unconsciously. At that time in my life, I had no conscious understanding of how I could observe my emotions without being subject to them (anyone who reads my whole journal would now be saying, "Ya' think??!!"). Yet even without understanding what I was actually doing, I acted from the place of compassion and understanding provided by my true Self rather than *re*-acting to the self-centered emotions of jealousy provided by a wounded ego. Yet even though I acted in a life-affirming way, I still saw that behavior as "really strange." When one learns how to consciously accept the identity of the true Self and act from that place consistently, then it is the *other* behavior that is seen as really strange.

Now let me be clear about something (well, hopefully I've been clear about a LOT of things but you know what I mean). Even the most enlightened Beings on the planet still FEEL emotions – and not just the bunny-hugging variety. Anger, fear, guilt, jealousy, lust, sloth, depression – the whole gamut. Thank God for that! We have emotions for a reason – to bring us information. In this case, the emotion I interpreted as jealousy was just telling me that I cared for Jo and didn't trust that this other guy wouldn't hurt her. Once I spoke to her and knew that she hadn't been hurt, that emotion was gone.

Just like our five senses, our emotions enable us to interact with other people, animals, plants, and circumstances. And our emotions are not limited, as our five senses are, to the area immediately around us. Some of us are more sensitive than others in this regard but ALL of us (if you are more than two days old) have at one time or another felt deep anger, sadness, or joy without being aware of why we were feeling it. Everybody knows somebody that can brighten up a whole room .... by leaving!! Conversely, and more pleasantly, we have those friends who seem to carry joy with them and your black cloud can lift just thinking about them or hearing their voice. All of this, and far more, is courtesy of your emotional realm.

In fact, without your emotions you would not be able to feel love, compassion, kindness, oneness, and all of the other blessings that make life so delightful. Spirit even uses the emotional realm to let us know when we are on the right track by filling us with something that is hard to define but unmistakable when present. One way it showed up in me is described in this entry:

July 13 – 6:30 PM

I may be in the midst of a really down period but I just realized how fortunate I am. I have previously referred to the tremendous inner feeling of independence and freedom that I feel at different times – especially when heading on the open road for a new city. Would that I were a writer so that I could phrase it with words better suited to do justice to that incomparable feeling. Today it came to me how few people ever get to experience that feeling. I can't help but think – in this, our 200th year – how different it must have been in the days of the pioneers and settlers. Not only did a much greater percent of the people experience this freedom, but it must have been much stronger then, also. They truly were a breed of people to be admired.

That "feeling of independence and freedom" mentioned above is really the feeling of being free from the binds of the ego state. It is that experience that I spoke about back in chapter 1 – the necessity to "leave thy father's house".

And the not-so-comfortable emotions like grief, sadness, anger, and envy all serve a purpose as well. They too are bringing us information. There are hundreds of books on the shelf that can bring you to a deeper understanding of how that information can be used by you in creative ways. That is not something that I will go into in detail. My goal here is simply to point out that our emotions are a wonderful gift and an intrinsic and invaluable (now why do "valuable" and "invaluable" mean the same thing?? And how about "flammable" and "inflammable"?) part of our makeup that helps connect us both to God and to our environment.

When we view our emotional realm as a tool in this way then we recognize that we are not intended to be subject to that realm. It is here to serve us – not the other way around.

When I was 14, I came home after school, came bounding in the door and entered the kitchen saying, "What's for dinner, Mom?" Not highly original I'll grant you but I was hungry, okay? I stopped mid-sentence as I heard my mother, who was facing the other way, blast somebody on the phone. Now you have to understand that my mother was not prone to emotional outbursts but she was letting fly like a drill sergeant who had just had his boot scuffed by a new recruit – including words that I had never heard her say. What this outburst was about is immaterial but if you ever meet my sister Carol, ask her how Mom got her prom dress made on time. Anyway, as I was trying to moon-walk my way back out of the room as quietly as possible, she turned, saw

me, and said ....
"Hi Honey, how was school today?" and had a nice smile on her face as she said it! Not a trace of irritation in her voice. Not the slightest shade of mad on her face. How could that be?? Well, I didn't know HOW she did it then, but it was obvious to me in that moment, that emotions, even "negative" ones, could be rightly used and channeled in a specific direction. If there is anger that needs to be directed at a specific person, there is no need to flatten everybody in a one mile radius with it. Nor is there any need to carry it forward into the moment after it serves us.

SPIRITUAL INSIGHT # 12: ALL emotions can be appropriately used, under control, and do not need to be unleashed in all directions like a destructive tornado.

This holds for "positive" emotions as well. Many a person has had a joyful, perhaps ecstatic, experience with another individual or an event, and gotten hurt or even killed moments later by stepping in front of a truck or careening through a red light while lost in joyous rapture and not paying attention to their current surroundings.

I am not suggesting that you shouldn't feel the fullness of joy, love, and peace when those emotions come to you. The same is true of grief, anger, and despair. Your emotional realm brings you messages for a reason – to be FELT and experienced and you wouldn't be living life to the fullest if you sold yourself short in this realm. But, as my mother taught me, you don't have to allow your emotions to control your actions when it is inappropriate to do so.

I get it – it's not always easy to just release or get on top of emotions when they come on strong. Certainly there are people who suffer from chronic and intense grief, rage, and depression and I would never trivialize their experience by saying they should just "get over it". They can however take positive steps in seeking out people who can help them in a deep and lasting way. For many of us, however, we simply allow our emotions to take control of our actions out of habit or because nobody ever showed us that it could be different.

Let me give you just one tip on how to get control over those pesky, negative emotions. I know you will find this hard to believe, but there are times when I get grumpy. Sometimes I can identify a particular thing or person to blame it on (even though it is really probably due to something else) and sometimes I don't know where it's coming from. Doesn't matter. There I am in the midst of it and I'm loaded for bear – just waiting for some poor unsuspecting soul to tell me to "Have a nice day." Or I could be having a pity party. And you can be sure I have a damn good reason for it! How could that cop write me a ticket when I was only going five miles over the limit!!?? I can't believe that my (son, daughter, wife, husband, friend, boss...) did that to me! How could my insurance company raise my rates when I haven't had a claim in 18 years??!! Woe is me. I've been so badly done by. The Universe is out to get me. Yadda, yadda, yadda.

The first thing I do in such a circumstance is recognize what is going on. My higher Self (Spirit) sees what my humanity is experiencing through the emotional realm. Then I look at it and see if I can tell what message this is bringing me. Maybe it will become obvious to me. If it does, my energy will turn to working with whatever I've identified in a creative way and the anger or self-pity, having done its job as a messenger, will dissipate. Maybe an example would serve well here. I was in relationship with a woman who also had a relationship with another man, a friend of mine. In church one Sunday, I noticed that she was sitting with him and I felt the pangs of jealousy arise in me. Why was she sitting with him and not me? As I felt the poison of anger and fear rise in my emotions, my higher Self saw the underlying message: I loved and cared for this woman. That clear impulse was being distorted into the emotions of jealousy and possessiveness. Seeing that, I consciously concentrated on the true feelings of love that I had for her AND him. In less than a minute, the jealousy was gone and I was restored to a place of peace within myself.

If the message being brought by the emotion does not become evident to me, then I can choose to recognize that this represents a HUGE pattern in the world and that what I'm feeling is connecting me with millions of people who may be experiencing a similar emotion at that same time. I therefore have a channel through which I can touch all of those people. What is it I want to send to them? Perhaps assurance, thankfulness, peace, love, or compassion. As I concentrate on that message, it reaches *my* heart first thereby dissolving the anger or self-pity in me.

But sometimes I just can't get myself to radiate love when I'm feeling like ripping somebody's arms off. In that case, my larger Self gives my smaller self (human ego) permission to indulge in the anger or self-pity but I put a time limit on it – usually 20 minutes. Then I concentrate on MAXIMIZING the experience. Make it ridiculous. I'm not only mad at that idiot that cut me off. I hate everybody! I'm mad at bunnies, chicks, small children with doe eyes, roses in full bloom, and Aunt Bea (for you youngsters, ask your Dad or Mom about the Andy Griffith show). If I'm in the pity pool, then I dive deep. EVERYBODY is out to get me! The mailman is probably throwing away my mail, except for the junk mail. The baker sees me drooling and tells me that the éclair in the case is reserved for someone else when it isn't. My neighbor won't share his Sports Illustrated Swim Suit edition with me. My team takes a knee at the end of the game at the 1 yard line because they KNOW that I bet on them to beat the spread.

When you really see how ludicrous your behavior is when taken to the extreme, and FEEL how it is affecting your own mind and body, it becomes easy to let it go. I usually end up laughing out loud, which gets me some funny looks and a few "Are you OK's." But that's a small price to pay to put my higher Self back in the driver's seat. When that is the case, those emotions aren't pesky after all. They are simply the useful messengers they were intended to be.

Possible Questions to Consider in Your Journal

- Think of a recent situation in which you allowed your emotions to control your actions. What happened? What message do you think that emotion may have been bringing you? What might you have done if your Higher Self was in control?

- Write about an experience you have had where "you" watched "yourself" behaving in some way that you knew was inappropriate. Who was the "you" who was watching and who was the "you" who was acting? Which one do you feel is your true identity – the true "you"? Did you change your actions once you saw it as inappropriate? If not, do you think you could change your actions next time?

- What engenders anger in you? Sadness? Terror? Envy or jealousy? What useful messages might these emotions be bringing you. How could you respond to this information without "taking it out" on those around you?

Chapter 6

By the Time I Get to Phoenix

Don't know what it is about song titles. Probably comes from the practice that my sister and I have about breaking into song anytime anyone says anything that is close to a line from a song.

In any case, I've decided that I WILL share with you an extended bit of my journal. Seems like the best way to give you a feel for where I was at (Mrs. Kettenberg, my 8th grade English teacher, would smack me for using that phrase!) in October, 1976 when I arrived in Phoenix. It will also serve to introduce you to Emissaries of Divine Light – a spiritual group that has had a huge impact on my life. In my journal entries, any references to Emissaries, The Ministry, and The Family all refer to Emissaries of Divine Light.

Besides, I think you might enjoy peeking into my life back then. Kind of like reading someone's diary. Maybe this won't be nearly as exciting as reading your sister's diary, which you have always secretly wanted to do, but it'll be better than reading those nine-year-old magazines at your dentist's office. Don't get TOO excited, though. I plan to edit out the juicy sexual stuff since I told you I'm not writing THAT kind of book.

Let's start with when I arrived in Arizona.

Tuesday – Oct 12, 1976 – Tucson

Here I sit in the lobby of the huge Student Union at the University of Arizona. I have slightly mixed feelings about being among all of this youth. For the most part, it is invigorating, and I feel like a part of it. Then, I realize that I'm not. I wonder how I look to these people. Am I just another student in jeans, moccasins, and a T-shirt or do I stand out as an imposter? I ought to take a poll.

I'm here while waiting for 4:00 which is when Bill said to come over. I really can't think of any place I'd rather wait. Think I'll finish *Breakfast of Champions*. I do think that campus life would agree with me.

Is University life really that much better – more aware – more alive? The people all seem so involved and meaningful. What happens to all of the questions and feelings of youth once out of college? How does the "world" swallow up all of this positive power and neutralize it? I think I'll just sit out here (I've moved to a courtyard now), read my book, and watch and listen to the flow of life around me.

Oct 13 – Wednesday – 4:00 PM – Phoenix

Well, I'm back to not knowing what I'm going to do. Tucson seems to be the place I should move to. Bill and his wife Mary are nice people, and I also met a chick there – Jenny. As stated earlier, the U of A is loaded with chicks and seems much more alive than the Univ here in Phoenix (ASU). That's where I am right now, and I'm not as impressed as I was in Tucson. I contacted the people involved with the commune here, and I'm going to a meeting there tonight. My initial feelings are that it won't be for me, but I'll keep an open mind until I have a fuller picture. I could always try it and then move to Tucson if it wasn't working.

After writing the preceding entry, I took a little nap on a bench outside in a courtyard and woke up to my first dust storm. It really wasn't all that bad, but it was incredible how the blue, blue sky became all sandy brown suddenly.

October 14 – 10:30 PM

Looks like I decided on Phoenix – at least for a while. I don't know if I'll fit in with this group in Phoenix or not, but I may as well expand my experiences by giving it a try. As it turns out, I won't be living in a communal house, although that's where I am now. They're being nice enough to put me up until I get a place. John Amey (the head of the group) has contacted a couple that he thinks will want me to move in with them. They've got the room and need the $, so it should work out. We'll see.

The house I'm in now has 2 guys (Michael and Rich) and 2 chicks (Debbi and Toren) and Debbi's little boy, Jason (3 years old). These 2 girls + many of the others I met last night are pretty good looking but one thing they are not is loose!! Hell it would be tough to get laid in one of these houses anyhow with 2000 people around. I don't know how these living arrangements are going to affect my sex life, but it can't be any worse than my 1st 3 months in Houston!

Tomorrow is job search day.

Fox has begun to feel good again. I put new mufflers in her today, and Monday she goes for a tune-up. Then, hopefully, she'll be running in top form again. Just the mufflers alone made a big difference.

October 17 – Sunday – 1:30 AM

I think I'm really going to enjoy being around these people – even if they *are* called Emissaries of the Eternal Light! [*Actual name is "Emissaries of Divine Light"*] Their basic concern is improving the quality of Life – as it exists now – not what happens after death! How you live your life is what counts – that's easy for me to relate to. Also – they are entirely involved with their beliefs – but as an integrated way of life – not a separate philosophy to be preached. They live real lives – go to concerts, work, play, eat, drink – probably even have sex! This is not a cult or an extremist group – just some people who feel they know a better attitude to live by – that "Life" <u>should</u> be capitalized and consists of Truth and Love and Light and is worth living for its own sake. Amen.

<u>October 19 – Tuesday – 12:00 Noon</u>

I've moved in with Don and Jean Liniger, and I think it will work out. My sex life may be hampered just a bit, but I've got all the comforts of home including <u>good</u> home cooking, no hassle about a lease or phone or utilities, and some nice folks to live with. Unfortunately, although the neighborhood is nice, there are some bastard kids around. At least, that's what I must assume. I've only been here 2 days; and at 4:30 this morning, my car alarm goes off for the first time in 3 years! By the time I got out there, whoever opened the door was long gone, but the door was still ajar. Actually Don woke me up. The alarm woke him up. I think the alarm woke up ½ the neighborhood! Probably scared the heck out of the kid that opened the door!! I would have loved to have seen his face. Thinking we were in a pretty decent area, I had left the car unlocked and the windows down. Somebody – presumably a kid – must have seen my C.B antenna base and figured I still had a CB, so he would relieve me of it. Better luck next time. I just hope the alarm convinced him to try greener pastures and didn't get him pissed off so that he'd come back some night to do some damage.

Speaking of Fox – I met a 1-in-a-million mechanic here in Phoenix. John Amey recommended a fella named Earl. The Fox was running very rough at low end, so I planned on tuning her up. Earl surmised that the problem was just in cylinder #6. Sure enough, he found that that spark plug had developed solid carbon closing the gap entirely and, therefore, not firing. He also checked out some other things for me and smoothed the idle out a bit. Then we went for a test drive. Total time – 1 ½ - 2 hours (most of that time, we were just bullshitting!). Total charge - $6.10!! Needless to say, Earl has earned all of my business while I'm here + a hearty recommendation whenever possible!

I'm still in the job hunting process. In fact, I sit right now in a lobby waiting to be interviewed for a route driver job. So far, no luck, but that's to be expected at this stage. Phoenix has a high unemployment rate, but I'm confident that I'll find something.

October 20 – Wednesday – 10:00 AM

Never got to finish yesterday. They called me in for my interview. Today, I'm waiting around for an interview for a job as a route salesman for a packaged deli food company.

Last night I took a ride up South Mountain with Harvey. It is incredibly beautiful up there. You have a panoramic view of the whole valley – Phoenix, Scottsdale, Tempe, and probably a half dozen other towns with all of their night time jewelry shining. It's really something.

October 25 – Monday – 9:30 AM

"This Ministry"....."Our Master"........."Heavenly Orientation"............
These terms rub against my consciousness like sandpaper over a file. The resistance is incredible! Yet, why should it be so? If the ideas of these people are to take with me, I'll have to overcome the built-up revulsion I've developed over the years to this type of term. And why not? They are only terms – nothing more than words. The way of life expressed here is entirely acceptable to me – desirable in fact. Even their concept of a God living through each and every individual as separate cells in a whole body appeals to me. And they are not even hung up on "concepts" as such. Develop your own illusion of the form that God takes and wear that if it's more comfortable. Anyway – I must be patient. I have only scratched the surface here and gotten the tiniest bit of soil under my fingernails. Until I am covered by it and become one with it, I won't know if this Truth is real for me or not.

On a more physical plane – Toren and I have begun a "relationship". Nothing has developed beyond huggy-bear, kissy-face but it seems inevitable.

Amazing how my frame of mind can be so different. Whereas at another time, I might just have sat down and written, "I started dating Toren – can't wait to climb into her pants and…" [*rest omitted to avoid an "X" rating*] – I don't feel like that person at all right now. Even as I thought about writing in that vein, the idea and the words repulsed me. It's strange how I bounce in and out of the realm of vulgarity and crudity (if that's a word). Sometimes it's "f– this" and "f– that" and at other times I'm searching for my best words and most exquisite manner. Of course, a lot of that is determined by my environment and who I'm with, but the strange part is how comfortable I can feel within either attitude.

<u>Same Day – 11:00 PM</u>

Funny how I can go 5 days without writing and then fill up 2 or 3 pages in 1 day.

Met a chick today, and awareness of something about myself set in. I'll go out with anyone (almost) that exhibits a willingness to go out with me. This girl at work, Bambi, made no bones about the fact that she'd like to date me; and so, I'm seriously thinking about taking her out. I mean – she's thin and not too good looking (bad complexion); but just because she let me know that she wants to go out, I'm giving it serious thought. That's crazy!! Hell – she doesn't even have her own place! Lives with her aunt!

Even Toren is an example of that – sort of. Granted – she's very nice, and I'm fairly comfortable with her, and she doesn't have a bad body, but why am I thinking about getting into a "regular" dating pattern with her? Primarily, I think, because she's there, and she's willing! Maybe there's nothing wrong with that but right now it strikes me as crazy.

Started my new job today – working as an "interviewer" for Fruit Juice Corp. I try to "sell" people on the idea of operating a pair of vending machines as a part-time business. I like it because I'm basically out on my own, see people in their homes, and there's no "closing" involved. I just explain the business and prep them for a 2nd "closing" interview which another guy does. I can work limited hours, and my commission is $150 for everyone that signs up. I should be able to sign one/week, and that's all the $ I'll need. I think I'll enjoy this.

Saw Samuel Avital (mime artist) tonight but not performing – just in a lecture-demonstration. It was interesting but I think most of it went right by me.

Whoa!! Before you grow porkchop sideburns and start wearing bell bottom pants and Puka shell necklaces, I better get you out of the 70s, at least for a breather. This might be a good time to observe how my thoughts kept jumping around from the highly-spiritual considerations of Life Eternal to the earthly considerations of finding a job, keeping the car running, and trying to realize my sexual fantasies. Perhaps you might recognize this pattern as one which inhabits **your** mind and heart from time to time. Or not. At least you recognize this as showing up in your cousin Fred's life. This apparent schizophrenia is merely evidence of the various aspects that make YOU up – at least the *earthly* you (we'll get to the "other" YOU in a later chapter). These aspects are physical, mental, emotional, and spiritual. These are all elements of who you think yourself to be; and so, it is natural that you will be drawn in various directions trying to fulfill the needs of your body, mind, feelings, and spirit. This is considered normal behavior. As long as your desires don't translate into actions that society has decided will earn you an extended vacation with minimal amenities and a roommate named Bubba, you can navigate through life with a reasonable degree of happiness. You might even be considered a pretty nice guy (or gal) who occasionally eats too many Krispy Kremes and has a harmless penchant for dating younger women (or men – or both). You might also have noticed how these attempts to meet the desires of all four aspects of myself have been yanking me around from pillar to post. In other words, they are controlling my mood, my thoughts, and my actions at times.

SPIRITUAL INSIGHT # 13: Chasing my apparent desires to find happiness will bring me exhaustion, confusion, and frustration but never lasting joy.

Temporary happiness may well come from a good meal, a funny movie, good sex, winning a game, an "atta boy" from your boss, buying a new car, lying on the beach, or thousands of other singular experiences. The happiness disappears, however, when the experience is over, or, worse, goes south when you get indigestion, lose a game, have a fight with your lover, get a poor review at work, get the first dent in that new car, or feel the sunburn from lying on the beach.

Joy is an internal experience that is not dependent on the outer circumstances. In fact, a joyous person extends that joy *into* his/her circumstances. It's like Craig, the 8 year old boy with no nose that I wrote about in Chapter 4. His joy comes from the inside out and is, therefore, a constant with him. What I have found in my life is that I can give up the constant attempt to make my body, mind, and emotions "happy", let the natural joy of my Spirit come forth ***through*** my body, mind, and emotions and, thereby, live in that space most of the time. I say "most of the time" because I haven't yet mastered staying there ALL of the time; but I'm only 65 now, so I figure I have another 60 years to get it right.

Going back to the exhaustion, confusion, and frustration mentioned above, let's continue with my journal and see how easily it comes up in chasing desires.

Oct 27 – Wednesday – 8:00 AM

Abstinence from sex will not be a problem much longer. Went out with Bambi (I told you I would!) for a drink after work last night and ended up with a kissy-poo, hands-all-over session in her car. If she weren't so tired, we would have spent the night together. Next time for sure. As to my previous entry – she really isn't bad. Although she is very thin, she's got decent boobs, and she is very cheerful. Bubbly personality – makes her easy to be with.

Oct 30 – Saturday – 10 Minutes Past Midnight

Went out with Bambi tonight, and I think I'm confused. We just went out for pizza and then back to her place. Her aunt and uncle were gone for the weekend, so we were all alone; but it was obvious that she didn't want to mess around at all – not even huggy-bear, kissy-face!! Could be something simple like [her menstrual cycle] but I don't think so. Maybe she's not as fast as I thought. Or she could have come on strong to get a dating relationship going. Or maybe she's a teaser. We have a date for dinner tomorrow night and at the very least I'm going to find out the story. [*Nothing further ever developed with Bambi.*]

Took Toren to the Fair last night. We had a good time, but that relationship baffles me also. She seems to enjoy herself with me, but somehow I feel she's not comfortable. What's worse – I'm not comfortable – and I'm not sure why not. The vibes just aren't smooth. If it continues, I'm going to talk to her about it.

If I don't hear from Carol tomorrow with some checks from TexCal, I'm in trouble. My $ here is depleted. I have $200 available to me as of Monday, but that goes to Nov room & board. My first paycheck isn't until Friday, and I already owe Rip (Toren) $20!! Every time I think I've seen the end of financial trouble, I'm in it again!!

<u>November 1 10:00 AM</u>

I've been thinking about Claudia a lot lately – ever since I've been in Phoenix – maybe before that. Is "absence makes the heart…" at work here? Do I really miss her, or is it just the absence of a good substitute? I might have really blown it this time. Not only has she found a new place to live and a whole new career – but also someone to share it all with. I've heard that she's living with Steve until she can find her own place and get her furniture shipped out. It's not improbable that they would grow very close and decide to stay together.

I probably will do nothing about it either. She loves me, and I know it; but I'm still not sure what my real feelings are. How could I call her and ask her to leave a whole new life for a question mark? Why should I even expect that she would?!!? Were I sure, I would join her in Chicago. That would be much fairer. I guess if I'm really serious even about finding out – giving it a try – that's what I should do.

<u>November 3 – Wednesday – 3:00 PM</u>

I'm kind of confused about my job again. What I'm doing now interests me because I'm out on my own – the hours are fairly short – the compensation is <u>potentially</u> adequate and more – and I enjoy talking to people in their homes without having to "close" them. <u>But</u> – I don't like working evenings, and I only make $100/wk if things don't work out. I'm investigating some other possibilities right now. As I write this, I'm thinking that I should stick with my present job and supplement it with substitute teaching if I can land that. We'll see.

Financially, everything's cool again. I got my TexCal checks from Carol right on time – the cavalry does it again. Even opened up a savings account!! Time will tell whether or not that'll grow or disappear again!

I've got racing fever again. I'll have to locate a club in the area and get into an autocross or something. Would also like to rally a little.

Socially – things are still fine: sexually – nothing.

<u>Same Day – 11:45 PM</u>

Body – you've got a helluva' challenge coming up in 8 hours. Tomorrow I spend 6 hours on construction – digging – with a shovel!! Hope I live through it!

Shared my first "attunement" tonight with Michael. As far as I could tell, nothing happened. I'm not even real sure what's supposed to happen!!

Bed time now – long day tomorrow.

<u>November 6 – Saturday - 9:00 AM</u>

I am experiencing difficulty in writing this – not emotionally, mentally, or spiritually – PHYSICALLY! Thursday I spent 6 hrs working with Lou on a jackhammer, and Friday, 5 ½ hrs by myself with pick and shovel!! Anybody got a 6' band-aid!!?? Hopefully, all of the muscle tissue will re-build itself over the weekend so I can go back to work on Monday!!

Meanwhile, back in the jungle, my other job is starting to gel. Two of my files closed and are now looking for financing. Be nice if they both went through. Leads have been slim lately though, so I've only got about ½ dozen open files.

I have started taking an "Art of Living" class sponsored by "The Ministry". It's Tuesday nights 7:30 – 9:30 for 8 weeks. That should help me get clearer insight or depth of feeling into what these people are all about. If things go well and my interest really develops, maybe I'll take a "short class" (1 month) or "long class" (3 months) on Sunrise Ranch in Colorado. That would be beautiful in the spring. I think it would be a neat experience, though I'd end up broke again. I should be able to put away some $ while I'm in Phoenix though, so we'll see how it goes.

I've also been getting these strange impulses to cash it all in, head for Chicago, and see if I could work things out with Claudia. Boy – this is a lousy time of the year to go to Chicago!!

<u>November 8 – Monday – 2:00 PM</u>

Sex doesn't seem to be all that important, somehow. Maybe it's just because it's been 4-5 weeks since I've had any and my awareness of what I'm missing has dulled. Maybe it's because of my awkward living arrangement. Whatever the reason, it just doesn't seem to be all that pressing. Be interesting to see how I feel about it after the first time I get laid here. That should get the juices flowing again.

I don't recall if I've mentioned the situation with Toren, but there's something strange about it. On the one hand, she seems to want to spend time together – on the other, I'm not really getting any vibes from her. She doesn't seem to be very affectionate and that may have something to do with it. I also feel uneasy around her somehow – like I'm unsure what to do, how to act, what our relationship is. Sexually, it's funny too. I get the feeling that she would like to go to bed but something's not right. Again – our respective living arrangements may have a lot to do with that.

November 9 – Tuesday – 11:30 PM

About an hour after my last entry, I drove Fox face first into the center divider on I-17. I don't want to dwell on it now, but I do want to record what <u>actually</u> happened so <u>I</u> don't forget it. Hopefully, I really learned something.

A guy cut me off <u>very</u> badly and, I think, intentionally. However – I avoided any accident, and <u>that should have been the end of the incident.</u> Only someone acting very foolishly and <u>not in their own self interest</u> would have purposely caught up to the guy in an adjacent lane and yelled "What the f– is wrong with you?!!" I did that – Stupid move #1. The other guy yelled back "F– you", and <u>THAT should have been the end of the incident!!</u> That was when I made Stupid move #2 – As I started going by him, I yanked the wheel to the right to semi-cut him off and then sharply back to the left to get back in lane – much too sharply – did a 90 degree left turn and drove into the wall.

The damage report is not in yet, but it will be extensive; and I will be without the car for quite some time. It is <u>not</u> a big price to pay <u>IF</u> I fully learned:

I CONTROL ME AND WHAT I DO. THE ENVIRONMENT DOES <u>NOT</u> CONTROL ME!!

Good time for a break, jump back into the present, and expand the lesson I learned while wrecking my Corvette:

SPIRITUAL INSIGHT # 14: My consciousness determines what controls my actions. That WILL be the environment if and only if I choose that option. The environment will NEVER be in control of my actions when I choose to be in Divine Identity. OK – This looks a lot like Spiritual Insight # 11 back in chapter 5. It was worth repeating in a little different way.

Since we're in Phoenix now, let me use an example of an experience I had during those years. It was dawn on one of those rare, bone-chilling mornings in Phoenix where a cold rain was being driven by a shifting wind. Because that weather was unusual, I wasn't dressed for it. A group of us had gathered to participate in a Medicine Wheel ceremony. Most of my attention was on my discomfort, yet I really wanted to be fully present for the spiritual experience. I shifted my consciousness into a place where I honored the rain and the wind and accepted my Oneness with it. With that change in consciousness, the discomfort was gone; and I was fully immersed in a sacred experience that lasted throughout the ceremony. The wind and the rain and my body were all part of that sacredness and there was no separation. It was the consciousness I accepted in that moment that totally determined my experience.

Now back to your regularly scheduled journal, continuing on the same page.

There are also 2 moral issues involved in which I have made the decision to do what I know to be inherently wrong:

1. There was a "witness" who confirmed in the police report that it was the other guy's fault. He had evidently also cut off the witness who got the plate # and gave it to the police. They will undoubtedly issue a ticket. The insurance company is satisfied that it was not my fault (which of course it <u>was</u>). I should just

tell it like it was, but I will not. Maybe it's not "right", but it does seem just.

2. There was some work I was going to have fixed prior to the accident which I think I can lump into the claim. I have decided to do just that if I can.

   [*Note: I am pleased to say that, before the trial, my Higher Self took control. I came clean with the police and insurance company. Remarkably, I did not get into legal trouble, and my insurance company still paid the bill! Ain't it grand when things work out?!!*]

November 10 – Wednesday – 10:00 PM

This will be a confused entry. I'm not even sure why I'm writing. I was just contemplating how T.V makes a mindless piece of furniture out of me – even when I realize it!! I really should force myself into getting into something creative. Not for a living or even for other people – just for ME!! Knitting would be better than that damn T.V. What hold does it have on me? Even as I write this, I can't stop from listening to it in the next room; and the Linigers are watching the NEWS, which I don't even like!

I got a letter from Kathy O. [*Old flame from 1971 in San Jose*] yesterday. It's amazing how we enjoy such a close relationship. Maybe it's good that we're so far apart. We are attuned on a spiritual level and a physical, mental, and emotional relationship might just get in the way. She is a beautiful person and I'm glad I know her.

Spent $13 yesterday on a phone call to Mel. Got a postcard from him and knew that he needed to talk with me. Felt good to talk with him. He is a good friend.

Did Hemingway ever write simpler than this??!!

I haven't heard from Joan. I will not write or call her until I hear from her. She may need my help but she's got to reach out. I'm done jumping in after her.

November 14 – Sunday – 11:00 PM

Time is really whipping by. I've been in Phoenix a month already. That's incredible!

I don't know what I'm going to do with The Ministry. I had a long talk with Toren today about it and from her response, I guess I'm where I should be at this time. It's just something that's going to have to unfold. The Art of Living class has been interesting and should get more interesting as we go on. I'm going to services on Wed and Sunday. I like a lot of the ideas they put forth and the theory of living they express, but I'm sure that I'm missing their central point – this idea of "heavenly heredity" and "heavenly orientation". Next time they have a week seminar, I'd like to attend it. Maybe then I'll be able to determine if there's something here for me.

The insurance co has approved repairs on my car and the parts have been ordered. It ran over $3000!! Since it'll be 2 weeks or more before the parts come in, the body man rigged up some headlights so at least I can drive it. Once the parts come in, I'll have to rent a car until it's finished.

I finally wrote to Claudia at the old address hoping it'd get to her. I wish I honestly knew how I felt about her. We certainly did have a good thing, and she would certainly make a good mate. I'll see what she writes back.

November 19 – Friday – 3:00 PM

I think this will be the last time I board. The Linigers are really nice, and I certainly don't have any complaints about them. There are also some strong advantages – especially good meals with no cooking, shopping, or cleaning up. In addition, there are always people around which eliminates one of the worst problems of living alone. For the long haul, however, I think I prefer my own castle. While I'm traveling though, I guess this arrangement will do nicely.

The main concept of The Family – that of only being able to find true peace internally – seems to make sense to me, and yet I can't shake the feeling that a couple is where it's at. Sharing things with a special someone else makes me a whole person – or so I believe. Maybe they're right. After all, I've found some dynamite chicks, but it's never been all together for me. Maybe the whole Truth of Life does have to come from within before you can really share wholeness with someone.

Did you catch all of the life lessons in there?? Well, I'm not going to review them all. I do, however, feel some responsibility as the author to at least try to present some grist for the mill. Let's take, for instance, the fact that the word "confused" appears in this segment of my journal three times as well as other references to confusion without using the actual word. One thing that I have discovered in the 34+ years since this journal was written is that confusion is a sure sign of misplaced identity. As indicated in Spiritual Insight # 14, there is always a choice as to what identity is accepted into my consciousness. When identified with Divine Identity, the truth of myself, there is never confusion. When I identify solely with the earthly plane – my physical, mental, and emotional capacities – then I experience more confusion than a drunk in a house of mirrors.

There is a simple reason for that. The mind approaches all situations using only the information available to it, which is always extremely limited. The emotions are always concerned with establishing some level of comfort and that frequently leads to impossible conflicts of internal interest. Let's take the situation described in my journal for November 3 at 3pm. Why am I confused?

To start with, my emotions are in conflict. I like some of the things about the job and dislike other things. Sound familiar? It should. It pretty much describes just about every situation in the known universe (and probably the unknown universe but we've got enough to deal with here). Even a hot fudge sundae comes with the nagging guilt of those damn calories. If we can land a man on the moon, why can't we come up with a zero-calorie hot fudge sundae (and don't even THINK about mentioning carob here!)?

Mentally, I'm considering only the small percent of the facts available to me. For instance, if I had known that the Fruit Juice people I worked for were crooks (which they were) and that I was helping to bilk innocent people out of $3000 each, do you think that might have had some impact on this decision? "Well, of course it would have" you are saying, "but you DIDN'T know that; and there may have been a lot more that you didn't know. We can only make decisions based on what we DO know. There is no other way to do it." Really? Have you already forgotten what we talked about (OK – what **I** talked about) in Chapter 2? Go back and read it if you have to. I'll give you a key word – ***intuition.*** I'm not suggesting we ignore the facts in front of us and those which we do know. Those are important elements in our decision making, but they are not the only elements. In fact, they are not even the most important elements.

Remember how we said that our emotions bring us valuable information? That confusion I was feeling about my job situation was telling me something. It may not have spelled it out for me, but it was bringing me discomfort; and I should have paid attention. Though my other five senses did not bring me any concrete data suggesting I should leave this job, my emotional sense did. It is like when dogs or children just sense that a certain person is not to be trusted. Sometimes the rational mind has to interpret emotional data and make what might seem to be an irrational decision. It is said that Sigmund Freud made all of his major life decisions by flipping a coin. He watched his **reaction** to the outcome and that told him what to do. Even if he thought he felt equally about the two choices involved, if he found himself saying, "let's go two out of three" after the first coin flip, he knew that the other choice was the right one.

Let's go back to the journal for a quick peek.

<u>November 28 – Sunday – 1:00 PM</u>

I'm beginning to think that I'm thinking too much. I can't help but think that I've lived much of my life in the "Emissary" manner without calling it that or attaching to it any of the 'religious' connotations. I've always thought that life should flow through me and that you could only really know life by experiencing and expressing it. I don't know much about heavenly orientation but if that's just a title for total living experience, so be it.

SPIRITUAL INSIGHT #15: Sometimes, there's a blank. Like now. I thought this would be a good time for a spiritual insight but nothing, seemingly related to the topic, was there. I could have mentally cranked something out (after all, I AM really smart!) but by leaving space, Spirit filled the void, providing this spiritual insight. When you let your mind rest, listen for your intuition.

I am betting that there are lots more valuable lessons in those journal entries but they will be different for different people anyway so only YOU will see what is relevant and meaningful for you. In that way, this actually is a SELF-help book. In point of fact, EVERY book is a SELF-help book because each reader reads it with his/her own set of lenses, concepts, and perceptions. No two of us ever read the same book in that regard, and no two of us ever learn the same lessons. So go back and read these entries again. This time forget about MY story and look for the message that's there for YOU.

<u>Possible Questions to Consider in Your Journal</u>

- Forget this chapter. Forget this whole book. Just write about whatever is in your heart right now. Don't worry. The questions following this will still be there for you when you come back.
- Now go back and read the journal entries in this chapter until you strike an emotional chord. Why did you react to whatever it was? Write about that until it clarifies for you.
- What is your experience with happiness? How is your experience of joy different from your experience of happiness?
- Reflect on a time when you chose a consciousness that transcended outer circumstances. If you can't think of one for yourself, have you ever witnessed that experience in someone else? Imagine how it would feel for you and write about that.
- If you have ever kept a journal or a diary, go back to it, open it to a random page, read it and see if you have learned any "spiritual insights" since then that you can apply.

By the Time I Get to Phoenix

Chapter 7

What Do You Say
After the Orange Juice?

SEX! See how that got your attention? Seems like I should have a chapter about it. I'm amazed by how much of my journal has to do with sex! Getting it, not getting it, wanting it, thinking about it, fantasizing - which is a good thing because everybody knows you can't have a best seller without sex!! Besides – I was 29 years old at the time, and it was the era of The Pill and prior to AIDS where everyone was having sex without guilt or worry. When I left NJ, I had the idea that juicy sex would play a big part in this book. Now, however, I'm older, wiser, and more mature (well, OK – older anyway), and I no longer want to write "that kind of book". Honestly, though, is there ANYONE out there who doesn't recognize that sex is a HUGE part of the human story – besides your Aunt Florrie who is still trying to convince you that you'll go blind.

Sex is a beautiful experience and a horrible experience – incredibly exciting and nail-filingly dull, over-anticipated and under-appreciated, scary, loving, crass, gentle, rambunctious, athletic – and I could go on, but I don't want to write that LONG a book. Suffice it to say that there is a huge range of sexual experience available to human beings. The idea for this chapter, for instance, came one morning (while still back in NJ) following a very enjoyable night of sex with a woman named Joan that I barely knew. This had been our first date. The next morning, she made a lovely breakfast. As I was drinking my OJ, I was thinking, "What am I going to say to this woman after I finish my orange juice?" I really had no desire to get to know her better even though we had just shared such an intimate experience.

That's when I realized that we hadn't shared intimacy at all. We had just had physical sex. That's all! Hit me like a shock wave – sex and intimacy are two separate things. Though they are joined during the highest form of sex, they are not synonymous. Two people can have sex all night (or for 20 years in a marriage) with no intimacy between them at all. Conversely, two people can share an intensely intimate moment without touching each other or even saying a word. I realized relatively early on that intimacy means more than physical sex, though the lure of physical sex is so strong. Consider this entry:

December 6, 1976 – Monday – 11:00 AM

I'm really not sure if The Family is for me or not. I could just be riding along with it to "belong" and avoid loneliness. Inside though, I feel like these people have really touched the truth. Maybe it's represented well in the area of sex. I've really been pre-occupied with it – maybe more than usual for me – which is a lot!! I've gone out with Toren and Sharon from

77

The Family, and they both express the same idea: forget the game and let life flow naturally. Sex will come (no pun intended!) when it is right and that will make it good. I think I really believe that, but a good part of me still reacts as I always have. I'm pursuing it on "the outside" from 2 sources – Karla and Lorraine. Met Lorraine on the road when I pulled up next to her and started to rap. She's 19 and is in the process of moving into the area. Haven't seen her yet, but I probably will next week. Neither of those situations is "right" for me. I recognize that, but I'll still pursue them just to get laid. Wonder if I'll ever reach a level of maturity where I don't do dumb things like this!! One of these days, I'm going to have to write that book – *What Do You Say After The Orange Juice?*.

Well – I never wrote the book, but at least I wrote a chapter with that name!

Somewhere along the way I had the realization that the relationship can make the sex good, but it doesn't work the other way around. I'm sure I'm not the only one who has been in a relationship that was, shall we say, less than creative even though the sex was great. In light of this revelation, I was sometimes able to see physical sex in a little clearer light – even if still fuzzy around the edges.

December 12 – Sunday – 10:00 AM

My chastity ended last night, and I have mixed emotions about it. Imagine that – after all that anticipation and wall crawling, I actually have mixed emotions!!

Facts: My partner was Susie – a girl from the office. Nice enough girl, but certainly not a dynamite personality - a little over weight and not good looking at all. We spent the evening watching T.V. and got it on 3 times.

Feelings and Observations: Physical sex can be an entirely separate realm. People who decide they must be in love because of a good sexual experience are tragically confusing things. The sexual activity I experienced last night was good and even the vibes surrounding it were good - warmth – close feeling – caring – gentleness – all of the good ingredients – even a fairly comfortable feeling afterward. The fact that all of that was there is what made it obvious to me that sex is a realm unto itself. This good feeling did not grow out of a close touching relationship, but just existed by itself. Of course, as such, it doesn't endure. Though a dynamite sexual relationship can stem from closeness, the opposite does not hold true. This is not to say that sex cannot come first followed by a solid relationship – but that the relationship grows independently of and sometimes in spite of the initial sexual activity. If a true closeness develops, then a closer sexual relationship will grow anew from the fertile soil of the shared oneness. Now I realize why sexual activity early in a relationship can be dangerous. It is not because it is wrong or immoral but because the physical and emotional feelings experienced can, too easily, be confused with similar feelings that grow out of a deeper, more meaningful relationship. Yet these feelings, based solely on sexual response, are shallow; and a shared life based on them has a foundation of loose sand. Unless a truer relationship develops in a natural course, the relationship must crumble.

I even found a way to talk about this in poetic terms while in Phoenix. Here is my offering from Dec. 26, 1977. It may not win any poetry awards, but I think you all might be able to relate a bit to the feelings involved.

The drive is so strong – Could it really be wrong?
It passes
Yes, it passes – but surely returns.
Like Sol, it gives Light, but also burns.

How can one thing be so Right – so pure
And so much an expression of that which is True.
Yet even as a pronouncement of Oneness,
So too an underlining statement –
> *Of Loneliness.*

Can I learn to control it,
To know when it's Right?
Now move with it
Express it
And now rein in tight.

What it is – let it be.
How to use it – let me see.

There are a VAST number of books about sex available everywhere from the Better Sex Book Club (don't look it up – I just invented it) to the plain brown paper wrapper type that I have only heard about. I would like to consider with you why it is that sex DOES in fact make the world go 'round. I also promise to tell you how to have the best sex you have EVER had – but that's in a later chapter. Right now, I want to consider sex on a much larger scale.

It was much later than that morning at the breakfast table with Joan in N.J. that I came to know that the sex principle runs the universe but that it is not limited to what I had always thought of as "sex". Think about it – why does the solar system hang together? There is a positive pull from the sun and each planet responds to that gravitational pull (I know there is a lot more to it than that, but this isn't a physics book so I'm taking author's license, whatever that is). So we have a positive force from the sun that we could call "radiation" and a reaction from the planets that we could call "response". As that *attraction* is maintained, a *union* is formed among the sun, the planets, and other heavenly bodies involved that we call the solar system. This body then becomes an extension of the sun at the center and, as a unified whole, extends the influence of the sun further out into the galaxy. This is an example of "unified radiation" where a radiant force and that which is responsive to it become one. This is true union, and it represents the sex principle: Radiation – Response – Attraction – Union – Unified Radiation. If it sounds familiar, you experienced it with your "first love" – whether in 6th grade with Nancy Wallace or at your 50th high school reunion with the one you never noticed during school daze.

It is perhaps clearly represented by bar magnets. What happens if one magnet is held firmly with the positive (radiant) pole facing in a given direction and another magnet is brought into that field? If the negative (responsive) pole of the second magnet is facing the positive pole of the first, there is strong attraction and union. The two magnets then become one with a unified field of radiation. If the positive pole of the second magnet, however, is facing the positive pole of the first, there is repulsion. Think about Mary Jo Friedlander's reaction when you asked her to the Junior Prom (Oops – sorry – didn't mean to open old wounds).

You may recognize that the same pattern exhibited by the solar system is pretty similar in the atom. I'll go out on a limb here and guess that you fit right in there someplace between an atom and a planet. We all do. So it's reasonable to assume that the same law that operates in both of those arenas works for us, too. That's why I came to know this principle as The One Law: Radiation – Response – Attraction – Union – Unified Radiation. Which brings us to:

SPIRITUAL INSIGHT # 16: Whatever you give your attention to expands in your experience; and if you continue to respond, you become one with it and that is reflected in your expression into the world.

Remember when you were a kid and you read in the Bible, "...and he knew her and they had children." Whoa!! Didn't they skip over a few steps??!! Later, of course, you learned that "knowing" someone in the biblical sense means that they had sex together. The fuller meaning is "to have union with" or "to be one with". So that which you have union with becomes that which you know in the fullest sense of the word. Facts are those things that we know *about*. That which we truly *know* is that which has become a part of our very Being.

I know – we've gotten away from talking about sex in the juicy way, but I told you this wasn't going to be *that* kind of book. Besides, have we REALLY gotten away from the juicy stuff? What could be more exciting than choosing that which will control your entire life?!!? That actually COULD be physical sex. In fact, it is for a lot of people. It could also be the pursuit of wealth, position, or power. It could be alcohol or drugs or food. It could be righteous indignation, patriotism, or the Arizona Cardinals (Oh sure it would have been easier to say the NY Yankees or Green Bay Packers, but give me a break; I'd spent 32 years in Arizona!). In fact, there are more "Anonymous" groups than horny teenagers in Texas (just trying to stay with the sex theme here). Why? Because people everywhere are drawn to "something," trying to fill a void that they feel inside. Problem is, they are turning their "negative pole," their response, to the wrong things. The country song had it right – "Lookin' For Love in All the Wrong Places".

So what should you be responding to in order to have a joyous, complete, fulfilled life? LIFE!! Other ways to say this would be God, the Universe, Yahweh, Spirit, Allah, the Higher Power, or any other words that you choose to represent that which is the constant expression of Love and Truth. And here's the good news:

> **SPIRITUAL INSIGHT # 17: That power – God – is within you and you are within God. It is not something external for which you have to search.**

Now don't get me wrong. I am not anti-sex – you know, the good old-fashioned kind involving frantic removal of clothes, sounds that would be embarrassing anywhere else, and copying positions from the Kama Sutra – but I am talking about something that is better than that kind of sex (no – not chocolate, although that's right up there). It is the principle that underlies what I described in Chapter 2: finding union with what you were born to do. It goes beyond your vocation, though that is a big part of it, especially in Western society where our work is such a big part of our lives.

Forget that amazing, explosive moment of sex for a minute even though that's hard to forget. Hey, it isn't called "climax" for no reason! Think instead about that feeling just after. That warm, endorphin-filled, satisfied, everything's-right-with-the-world feeling. Now imagine feeling like that ALL THE TIME. Well, maybe not exactly like that but with that kind of calm peace and joy. That's what it's like when you open up and find union with God's design of Life for you.

It's not as much about *what you do* as about *what you express* while doing what you do.

At some time in your life you have asked the question or at least fleetingly thought to yourself, "Who am I REALLY?" What I'm talking about here is not only knowing the answer to that question but expressing it in ways truly natural to you so that EVERYBODY sees the answer to that question. When people say, "She was born to dance" or "He is a natural lumberjack," they are not talking about the skill the person is exhibiting as much as the *love* with which they are doing it. That person has found union with his/her calling and is letting the world see his/her true identity. That identity is not the dancing or the lumberjacking (is that really a word?). It is the LOVE that they express while doing those things. This is what I call Divine selfishness - doing what brings you the greatest fulfillment in life – experiencing and expressing union with the Truth of your Being.

MORE GOOD NEWS: Once you find that expression, you can allow it to come out in everything you do – washing the dog, driving your car, shoveling the walk (you Arizona and Florida people will have to look that one up) and even paying the overdue bills.

Living in that place means that you really will know what to say after the orange juice – no matter what the sex was like.

Possible Questions to Consider in Your Journal

- What has your experience been with both sex and intimacy? After writing about that for a while, write a poem regarding some aspect of what you have written. For those who don't think they can write poetry, remember three things: 1. It doesn't need to rhyme. 2. Nobody is going to read it unless you show it to them. 3. We are all creative beings. Just bring a situation to mind and start to write. See what comes out. You can always burn it!

- How have you seen the "One Law" work in your life? Think of two different scenarios – one in which you were responding to something other than God (an addiction, bad influence, misguided authority figure, etc) and one in which you felt that you were clearly open to Spirit. How was your expression out into the rest of your world affected? What was the impact on your physical, mental, and emotional health?

- Write about what it feels like when you are doing something that feels natural and right. What is the impact on your body, thoughts, and emotions? How would your life be affected if you brought that feeling and expression into everything that you do?

Chapter 8

Emissaries of What??

In the last two chapters, I had mentioned, usually in my journal entries, a spiritual organization named Emissaries of Divine Light (EDL). Since I did mention them and they have been a huge part of my life ever since then AND most of the spiritual insights included in this book came to me through my association with EDL, it would be remiss of me not to say more about them. I won't go into detail about the logistics of the organization. You can find all of that and a great deal more at www.emissaries.org. What I would like to talk about is what this organization means to me.

But before I go there, I want to honor the two people that I consider my first spiritual mentors – Jack and Ruth Pearlman. If you are sharp, you may have noticed a similarity in our names. I never called them Ruth and Jack. I called them Mom and Dad. I've already given you one lesson I learned from my Mom back in Chapter 5 – Spiritual Insight # 12: "All emotions can be appropriately used, under control, and do not need to be unleashed in all directions." If you don't recall the story, go back and read it. You will see that I did not learn this lesson by Mom sitting me down and explaining it to me. In fact, I didn't even realize that I HAD learned that lesson until several years later. Whoever said, "What you do speaks so loudly that I can't hear what you say" hit it on the head. Usually that is used in a negative way, but it also applies in a positive way. We reveal ourselves ALL THE TIME through our actions. In this particular instance, my mother was teaching me a great Truth without once saying a word about it. In fact, she was probably not conscious of teaching me anything in that moment. That is true of virtually everything of value that I learned from my parents.

Another example: When I was a senior, Hillside High introduced a new experimental Calculus class on a voluntary basis. The grade you got would not appear on your transcript nor affect your cumulative average. We were told that this class would be taught at a very high level with no consideration given to those struggling. 26 students signed up to take it and an exam was given to all of us to test our retention of our past math classes: algebra, geometry, trig, etc. Based on the results of that exam, 21 of the 26 were advised not to take Calculus. My friend Lonnie and I each scored an 18 on the exam, the lowest score registered, and we were among those advised to drop it. Lonnie did. I went home to talk to Mom about it. After hearing all of the facts as I explained them to her, she simply asked me what I wanted to do. I told her that I felt it would prepare me for my Engineering college curriculum and that I wanted to take it but that the teacher felt that I would probably fall behind and fail. She asked me if I thought it would still be a valuable experience even if I did fail the course. When I answered that question, I knew what was right for me to do. She never had to say the words. I took the class, earned a C, and breezed through Calculus the next year during my freshman year at Rutgers while many flunked out of the Engineering curriculum based on flunking Calculus.

> **SPIRITUAL INSIGHT #18: Regardless of external factors, look inside yourself and you will always know what is right for you to do.**

This insight comes with a caveat. You have to be in a clear space to truly look inside yourself and actually see anything. How do you get in a clear space? First, you have to come past the emotions. I find it impossible to have any clear spiritual vision when I am being controlled by my emotions. Kind of reminds you of when you were advised to count to ten before acting out of anger, doesn't it? In this case, the emotions I was feeling were doubt, fear, and a bit of anger. My mother acted as the vehicle to guide me in a process that allowed those emotions to subside and bring me to that clear space that allowed me to access my inner wisdom. At the time, I saw her as the wise one, although she was wise enough never to present herself that way. She just helped me to see what I already knew.

I'm 65 now, and Mom and Dad are long gone. For decades before they died, they ceased being directly involved in my decision-making process. The process that I use to this day, however, is the one that my parents taught me (the Calculus example is one of many I could have cited with either my Mom or Dad) without being aware that they were teaching me anything – or - maybe they were aware, and I just never knew it. So how do I do it now? Sometimes a trusted, wise friend takes the place of my parents. Sometimes I journal or find a quiet place to just let my mind and heart be at peace. (I like the woods or the beach or a mountaintop, but I know people who go running or take a bath or work in the garden. In fact, I have a friend who told me that he would do this as a matter of survival while flying a jet fighter during the Viet Nam war! The quiet place, after all, is IN me – not necessarily around me.) However you find your way there, you MUST get there in order to access your Truth.

Parenthetically (another one of those cool six syllable words publishers like), how you come to recognize this Truth is as individual as how you come to a clear space. Some feel it in their bodies. Some have a vision. Some hear an inner voice. You might use Freud's coin-flipping method described in Chapter 6. I just KNOW without being able to describe how. Don't expect it to come to you in any specific way. Just stay open and aware of what DOES come to you. Then be willing to follow your guidance, even if it is hard.

Paul, a good friend for many years, had been a vegetarian for at least three decades. It was one of the sacrosanct principles on which he based his living. Paul was very knowledgeable about natural healing. One year he became ill and, regardless of his treatments, he continued to go downhill. He took a walk in the wilderness to meditate about it, and the guidance that came to him was that he needed animal protein in his body. The thought horrified him. He continued to meditate on it over several days. He finally came to the conclusion that the choice he faced was to be controlled by a principle that *had been* true for him for many years or by the truth as it was being revealed to him in the present moment. He said it was one of the hardest decisions he ever had. He chose to add small amounts of turkey to his diet and regained his health.

I can't leave Dad out of my examples of spiritual lessons learned. Picture this. I'm a freshman at college visiting home on spring break and at the library doing research for a paper. I've borrowed Mom's car and suddenly realize that I have 10 minutes to get home to return the car on time. Zipping along the streets of Hillside at something approaching twice the speed limit I see Officer Friendly pass me going the other way and then turn his motorcycle around to get behind me.

Knowing he is about to turn his lights on, I start to pull over. That is the moment that my rational mind went on vacation, and I began to channel a combination of Pretty Boy Floyd and Richard Petty. Instead of stopping at the corner, I whipped around it and began a chase through a residential neighborhood that saw me run stop signs, drive over sidewalks, over somebody's lawn, and, when I had turned enough corners that he was not in line of sight anymore, behind someone's house. To this day, I firmly believe that there was one traffic law I didn't break; but I haven't yet found it in the manual. Only Divine Providence kept me from hurting or killing anyone that day. While still operating on finely honed stupidity, I jumped out of my car and ran into a backyard shed, thinking that the officer would probably miss the subtle clue of the tire track ruts in the man's yard. Unfortunately, his Sherlock Holmesian powers of observation picked up that minute detail, and the next thing I heard was "Come out with your hands over your head." My adrenaline level did not go down when I saw a very angry police officer with ripped pants and a bleeding knee acquired when he had laid the bike down while chasing me. Looking down the barrel of a large bore weapon, I felt like I was on the wrong side of a Dirty Harry movie, and I wasn't planning on making his day. Once he was convinced that I was just incredibly stupid and not dangerous, he put the gun away and started writing tickets. I believe he is still in the Guiness Book of World Records for most citations written to a single individual in one day.

What has this terribly amusing story got to do with my father? We're getting there.

They impounded my car to search it for drugs or evidence of other crimes since it was hard for anyone to believe that I would run from a police officer just because, as I was quoted in the paper saying, "I had too many tickets and didn't want to get any more." I was booked for breaking and entering (did you know that you don't actually have to "break in" to a dwelling or shed to be charged with "breaking and entering"?) and interrogated by two police officers for a while. Then they said the magic words that truly struck fear into my heart, "We've called your father. He's here now, and he's asked to speak to you alone." Now you have to understand that the only time my father had ever hit me was when I was mad at him and chose to get even by crying into my mother's mink coat, which had just been brought home from the dry cleaner. When he heard noise in the closet and saw what now looked like a rat's nest, his primitive instincts took over but even then it was just one slap – nothing to warrant a call to Child Protective Services. That had been ten years earlier. So there was no real reason to justify my desire to be locked up rather than have to be alone in this room with my father, but that's how I felt. A small part of me was afraid he would kill me, but most of me was just so ashamed that I had let him down like that. What happened surprised me. He sat down and softly asked me what had happened. When I explained that I had just done the stupidest thing in my life and had no rationale for it whatever, he put his hand on my shoulder and simply said, "Well, let's see what we have to do to get you out of here." Then we went to talk to the officer in charge who considered my totally clean record and agreed to drop the felony breaking-and-entering charge. He totaled up my fines, took my license, and let us go home. We never talked about it again. He knew that I had learned the lessons to be learned and had already punished myself.

SPIRITUAL INSIGHT # 19: When someone acts out of ignorance, find a way to pick them up, not knock them down further.

I could tell stories about my parents all day long (all book long?); and, if you ever get around my brother, sister, and me at the same time, we probably will, but since this chapter is named after the Emissaries, it seems only fitting that I say a few words about that organization.

When I first stumbled upon Emissaries of Divine Light, in the same synchronistic way that I stumbled upon my sales career, I didn't know anything about them except that they had a communal farm in Oregon, a few communal homes in Phoenix, and that they were having a meeting the same night I got to Phoenix. At the time, I knew that I was searching for something and that it had something to do with God, but I wasn't at all sure that I was going to find any answers here. I would have been happy to have continued my adventure and, hopefully, found a sexual partner. As you read in chapter 6, however, I soon recognized that the principles espoused by the Emissary philosophy rang true to me. In the early days of my association with EDL, I was a bit put off by the name: Emissaries of Divine Light. I mean, HELLO – might as well put up a sign that says "I am a member of a cult"!! Nevertheless, I have grown to really appreciate that name, because I see it as being an accurate description of what I am and, in fact, what I had always been: one who has come to represent the Truth of God. We are all meant to be that. Don't panic – I'm not trying to get you to join anything, because I don't believe that everyone is meant to be an Emissary of Divine Light with capital letters, meaning a member of an organization. We ARE each meant to be an emissary of divine light with small letters (although I must admit it was hard for me to not capitalize "Divine"), meaning people who recognize their Divine (see – I couldn't do it again!) nature and their responsibility to bring Heaven into the earth by sharing Truth, Love, and Life with their fellow human beings and all other life on the planet. Why should I feel self-conscious about giving myself THAT label? So, I have been an emissary of divine light my whole life and an Emissary of Divine Light for the past 35 years or so.

What has that meant for me? It has meant continually looking deeper into myself to find how that Truth, Love, and Life is meant to appear through me. I was always grateful that my spiritual mentors in the Emissary program never asked me to "toe the party line" in any way nor to accept anything in faith but rather to test anything that I heard from ANYBODY against what I knew to be true when I was in that quiet place of wisdom that I spoke about in the beginning of this chapter. I participated in a two-month class with the Emissaries in 1979. At the end of that class, our primary facilitator, Michael Cecil, suggested to us that we burn all of our notes, always act only from what we really KNOW to be true, and never to accept something as true just because he, or anybody else, said it.

The man who was the head of the Emissary program during my first 13 years associated with the Emissaries was Martin Cecil (later known as Martin Exeter – a title as an English Lord that he inherited when his older brother died). Though I didn't then, and don't now, fall down to worship him, he was perhaps the wisest, most spiritual man I ever knew. I found his words incredibly insightful and true in my heart; but, like my parents, I learned more by observing his living then I did from his words. I was also fortunate to be mentored by John and Carol Amey – the couple who were the "primary focalizers" (read: "Big Kahunas") for the Arizona Emissaries. John is a big, no-nonsense guy (miner when growing up and lawyer turned Arizona Assistant Attorney General for decades) who tells it like it is but is totally surrendered to God in his life. Carol is Mother Nature in earthly disguise. She has the greatest affinity for all life - animals, plants, minerals, and people – of anybody I have ever met. You feel like she could resurrect the dead if she knew it was the right thing to do. Both have hearts too big to measure, and you couldn't find better friends. John knew I was destined to lead the Arizona Emissaries long before I did, and Carol knew that I was a poet and singer even while I was telling her that I MOST definitely was not!

A few years after I arrived in Phoenix, John and Carol moved to Sunrise Ranch, the Emissaries' International HQ in Colorado. My wife Mary (bit more about my marriage in the Epilogue) and I took over as primary focalizers in Arizona.

Once more, I am going to tell you that this isn't what this book is about. I did want to say just a bit about my spiritual background with my parents and with EDL, and I think what I've presented here is sufficient for now. I will say that the Emissaries have been active since 1932 with the stated intention of the spiritual regeneration of the human race under the inspiration of God. If you are feeling like there has been something missing in your life – whether your life has been great or something less than great – and you want to find out more about what's been missing, it would be a step in the right direction to contact EDL through the Web site I gave earlier in this chapter. And don't forget to use my name. If you combine that with $4, you can get a cup of coffee at Starbucks!

I wasn't going to include any Emissary services as a part of this book, but I just changed my mind again. I know - all this time you thought that writing a book was a logical, orderly procession of ideas within a structured linear framework. Maybe for some, but not for me. I'm not sure that this totally fits, but I'm feeling moved by Spirit to include one of the services that I gave during this time in Phoenix. While Martin was alive, we would receive recorded transcripts of the services that he gave, extemporaneously, every Sunday; and we would read them for our Sunday service time. Sometime after his death, I started to offer my own services in Arizona which were based in part on themes developed by the Emissary leadership the week before. Here is the transcript of one such service. I include it to give you a feel for the type of thinking that I feel is representative of the Emissary philosophy. This, by no means, covers it all but at least touches a toe into the ocean.

Welcome to the Real World
January 12, 2003

In a class I was recently teaching, I needed to evaluate sales reps based on their participation in role plays. I had to take into account that I was seeing them in an artificial environment and that I would be making my judgments based on how they were acting in an unreal situation, allowing for the fact that they might act significantly differently were they in a real-world situation.

That got me thinking about whether or not I provide a context of reality for the people that are in my world so that they can express themselves in a true way. When I say "a context of reality," what I think of is the reality of spiritual expression, which requires radiation and response. So if somebody is in my world and they're interacting with me, the question that I have to ask myself is, "What am I doing to provide a context of the truth of love, which is the truth of God's expression, so that there can be something real to respond to, providing a connection for spiritual expression to happen?"

If neither of us does that, then there is no true context of reality. What we tend to call the real world is actually the unreal world, but it is the world in which most people operate; and it's the world in which they know their own expression. The expression of the truth of them may not actually be in evidence that often. Well, is there anything or anyone there that they can respond to so that there can be the connection, so that it has a way to be present?

I heard a story of a man who was in the Far East for years studying Aikido. He had achieved a certain level of mastery. While on a subway car, he observed a large, powerful man who was drunk and abusive and terrorizing people on this car. The young man was considering how to handle the situation as the drunk faced him and was about to attack. An old Japanese man had been watching this whole thing and, as the bully prepared to charge, called to him softly with an invitation to come sit next to him. He did, and within minutes this guy, who just a minute ago was terrorizing everybody in the car, had his head on this old man's shoulder and was just crying his eyes out. They were sharing something in depth at a heart level.

The young man who was telling the story found out later that this old man sitting there was a highest-level Aikido master. He told the young man, "I saw you preparing yourself to handle violence with violence. That's not what Aikido is about. You need to connect heart to heart, and the violence will go away."

Here is an example of a person who was aware enough to know how to provide a context of reality when viewing a situation based in unreality, even though the participants felt like this was the real world. The old man knew the *real* world and invited others into it. When I do that, you have a context in which to express the reality of yourself, like this man did.

I have been aware at times of watching somebody, particularly in a service on a Sunday, express something in response that is beautiful and true. Yet, somebody else at another time commented that she felt that the person was being hypocritical, because that expression didn't match his expression in "real life". I would suggest that the expression she observed in what she called real life was, in fact, the hypocritical expression, and what was seen during the service pattern was the truth of whom the speaker is. The responsibility that we each have, whether we're in a service pattern or elsewhere, is to bring that context of the truth of reality, the truth of whom we are, the truth of the love of God, into our current situation. In this way, anyone in that situation has something to connect up to, as this man did on the subway with the older man, so that the individual can recognize and acknowledge the truth, the real world, and express himself accordingly.

Ideally, everyone would bring that context with them. Radiation and response, as we know, really is one thing. As we respond to the radiant point of life, we become one with that and move into the position of unified radiation. The response and the radiation are one. It's not sequential. It's simultaneous. Ideally, each person on the face of the earth would be that radiant point and would carry that context of reality with him/her, so that in any meeting between any two or more people there would be that context present, and true spiritual expression would result. I need to accept the responsibility to provide that context at all times.

My brother told me a story about two men walking their dogs, a Doberman and a Chihuahua. Deciding they would go into a restaurant, the man with the Doberman was stopped at the door and told the doorman that he was blind and needed his guide dog. Watching the success his friend had, the second man tried the same thing. The doorman disdainfully said, "Sir, they don't use Chihuahuas as guide dogs." To this he replied, "They gave me a Chihuahua?!"

In this instance, the man with the Chihuahua knows (a) he has a Chihuahua and (b) Chihuahuas are not guide dogs. Yet, he makes a choice to pretend that he doesn't know that in order to get what he thinks he wants. "All right, I want to achieve this goal to get into this restaurant. There's no way I can do it with the facts the way they are, so I'll pretend the facts are different."

That's choosing a context of ignorance. Well, I think that people frequently make the same choice. They choose a path that says, "I don't really know the truth." Now, they don't say that consciously to themselves. At a deep level they realize that if they really acknowledge the truth of themselves, it may not get them what they think they want. By pretending that they don't know the truth, they hope to achieve their desired goal.

Somewhere along the line, somebody has to bring a context of true reality to that person's experience, if they are, in fact, going to realize their greatest fulfillment. This is based in acknowledging the truth of whom they really are rather than denying it or pretending it doesn't exist. Somebody has to bring the context of life into focus. In this case, it was the doorman of the restaurant–although the analogy breaks down quickly, so we won't go there!

When we meet with people who have no conscious awareness of whom they really are, then, in that communication and in that interaction, we have to bring an awareness of whom *we* really are. This is an awareness of whom everyone really is–the oneness of the body of God on earth. We need to bring that awareness into that interaction for it to be present. If that light is present, if that context is available, then that person has the opportunity, at least, to connect up with it, to acknowledge it, and to move down that path. It doesn't mean it's going to happen, but it can.

We, on the other hand, don't have to know what that path is going to look like. It's not a question of coming into somebody's life and saying, "I know what Debbie should do; therefore, I'll provide all this wonderful light and she will do what I want her to do," or what you think she should do. No, it's not a question of deciding what that is for somebody. It's merely providing the context that each can come into so that *he* can have the vision for what is appropriate for him.

When you provide a context of light, you don't merely reveal to the person that they have a Chihuahua rather than a Doberman. You make them aware that they are not blind! They *have* vision. They *can* see. They *do* know who they are. They *do* know why they are on earth. They *do* have a connection with purpose, and they *can* follow a plan - not my plan, but the Divine design. This will come naturally through them once they open their eyes and accept reality. That's what we actually reveal to folks when we point out to them that "you've got a Chihuahua that you're following here, and it's not what you should be following." So vision is obviously important.

Also important is the ability to listen, to listen to our heart, to listen to that still, small voice, as Martin put it, and to actually hear. In a recent service that Cliff Penwell gave, one sentence jumped out at me. He said, "When we truly listen, we take a chance on losing our agenda in that answer." What we hear doesn't necessarily sound like what we were hoping it would sound like! It doesn't necessarily show us the next step that we were hoping it would show us. Then we have to make a choice: Do I follow what I just heard, which I think is clear and to the Tone, or do I follow the agenda that I already have?

When that still, small voice tells us something, it doesn't always come with all the details. It doesn't come and say, "This is what you need to do, and here's why, and here's why it makes more sense than this, or here's why it's going to fit." It doesn't always come that way. Sometimes it does, but in any case we have to make that choice. Do I have faith in what I hear from that still, small voice, or am I going to just say, "Nah, it doesn't make much sense to me"?

I train sales people to listen, but I also train them on how to set and follow out an agenda. The agenda, in our case, is geared towards selling our product. If you follow this agenda, and if you do it right, you can sell our product. The real goal, however, in every case is to reveal, both to myself and to my customers, what their real needs are and to provide them a path to accomplish their needs in the best way for them–whether or not it involves buying my product. That's the ultimate goal.

The agenda doesn't always match the goal. I don't know if they're going to match until I listen. When I go to those customers and really spend time with them and really open my ears and really listen to how they do business and what they want and what their goals are and where they're trying to get to, it becomes very clear to me, if I know what my product is, whether or not my product is going to help them meet their needs. If it will, then my job is to blend the path they present to me with my agenda which leads to the ultimate goal, the satisfaction of their needs.

If, however, it becomes apparent to me, while I'm listening carefully, that where they want to go is not where my agenda would take them–that in fact my product and my service is NOT the best thing for them–then I need to be prepared to drop my agenda and go back to achieving the real goal. This might involve sending them to one of my competitors or not changing anything. It might be showing them how to use their existing system to accomplish what they're trying to do.

The **real** goal is the generation of spiritual expression in the interaction that I have while we're going on whatever path we're going on. I have had many experiences of a beautiful generation of spiritual expression between me and other people which did not result in me selling anything. From a corporate standpoint, they might consider that a failure. From my purpose-on-earth standpoint, however, it was a great victory. That can also happen when they *do* buy. It doesn't matter if they buy my product or they don't buy my product. The question always is, "What was the purpose that was met by our interacting over these last few weeks, few months, or whatever it's been?" If it was the generation of spiritual substance, then my purpose was served.

The context is more important than the content. If I provide the appropriate context in any interaction that I have for any reason, then it allows for the possibility of spiritual expression to happen. The content of how we get there doesn't really matter. In terms of my profession, I might make a sale or I might not. The customer may agree with what I have to say, or they may not. It doesn't really matter.

A friend, Lou, recently got into an argument with a friend of his over the rules of a card game. That's content. If one gets so carried away with having one's way in content, the context is lost. If we can just agree that the reason we're playing cards is...and most people wouldn't say "to generate spiritual expression,"… but to have a nice time together, then who cares which rules we use. I'll do it your way, you do it my way, or we'll do it some other way. We'll make up our own rules. Who cares? Let's just enjoy the company. Children often just make up rules as they go, because the point is not who wins or loses. It's just to play the game and spend time together.

Well, we understand that, because we understand that we're here to provide context. The content can be whatever it needs to be so that the purpose of the context is met. This is providing the new heaven so the new earth can appear. Whatever comes out of it in terms of the new earth, in terms of actual activity, in terms of actual physical presence, is determined by the heaven that is set. I have to take the responsibility, in any interaction with anybody, to provide the heaven.

Now, that other person may be doing it just as well. In fact, at times, it's even more difficult when we're with somebody who, in our vision, does provide that. At times that we were with Martin or are with anybody that we feel provides that heaven, we may abdicate our responsibility. "Oh, well, I'm with Cliff Penwell, and Cliff provides that so well, so I'll just let him do it, and I'll come into response to him." There may be something to finding out who is in focus for a particular event and offering response to that. We never forget, however, that response and radiation is one thing and that I am responsible for providing the context, along with whomever is in focus. If we both do that, then there is a powerful context of spiritual expression and unified radiation.

That is one of many services that I gave in Phoenix, and I think it illustrates many of the principles taught by Emissaries of Divine Light. If you really liked it, let me know. Maybe my next book will be a compilation of my services. Speaking of which, there are three incredibly wonderful books that are compilations of services offered by Martin Cecil. They are called *Being Where You Are, On Eagle's Wings,* and *Beyond Belief.* Not sure you'll find them on Amazon or in book stores. If you don't, you can order them on the Emissary Web site, www.emissaries.org.

I know – some of you are still hung up on that name, Emissaries of Divine Light, so let's go back to the "cult" thing. Those of you who don't have any trouble with the name can skip this part and move on to the next chapter, although you might want to at least check out the Spiritual Insight up ahead.

"Cult" is defined as:

1. A particular system of religious worship, especially with reference to its rites and ceremonies.
2. An instance of great veneration of a person, ideal, or thing, especially as manifested by a body of admirers: the physical fitness cult.

Based on the second definition, virtually every group can be a cult: the Catholic (or Baptist or Mormon or any other) Church, the Republican (or Democrat, or Libertarian, or Green) Party, Yankees fans, Right to Lifers (or Pro-Choice people), Corvette Clubs, and Knitting Clubs (although I will admit it's hard to find a knitting cult). What makes a group a cult is the consciousness of "great veneration" by the people relating to the group. It doesn't mean that the whole group is a cult, although it can be. It means that the individual's behavior has become cultic towards that group. In itself, "great veneration" is not a bad thing but when a person stops thinking for him/herself, turns the responsibility for their life over to someone else, and substitutes dogma for the direct connection they have to the wisdom of their own God-Being, then it has become a cult for that person in the negative sense. So, is the Emissaries of Divine Light a cult? No – but that doesn't stop a person from relating to it in cultic consciousness. As careful as the Emissaries have been since their inception in 1932 to NOT create a carved-in-stone dogma, there have been, and may still be, people associated with the Emissaries who have insisted on creating one for themselves and then turning their lives over to that self-created, Emissary-labeled dogma. Know anyone in your church, political party, PTA, sports team, or social class who has done that? If you said "no", your group consists of all extraordinary people or you may be looking through rose-colored glasses.

SPIRITUAL INSIGHT # 20: In every moment of your life, you are being controlled by something. The most important thing you ever do is to choose carefully and consciously what that something is. That decision determines your entire life experience.

WOW!! Sounds like a biggie, doesn't it? Well, it is. Think of the times that you have acted under the control of anger, jealousy, fear, or depression. Think about when you have moved forward based on majority opinion or peer pressure, even though deep inside you didn't feel right about it. Or when you based decisions on the guidelines of other people or an organization without even giving it any independent thought. I'll bet that most of those situations did not work out in a way that felt personally fulfilling. When you accept the control of the Spirit of God as it is revealed to you in any given situation, the road chosen may not be easy or comfortable, but you will know that it is the right thing to do and that IS fulfilling.

Possible Questions to Consider in Your Journal

- Who have been your spiritual mentors? What did you learn from them? How did you learn those lessons?
- What guiding principles have you accepted in your life that you have tested against your own inner knowing? What principles have you discarded after finding out they were no longer true for you?
- Is there a current situation where someone you know has done something destructive in their life? Have you been doing anything to knock them down further? How can you help pick them up?
- What does it mean to you to develop a "context of reality" in your interactions with your friends, family, people at work, and others?
- Have you ever developed a cultic consciousness within a group or organization? What was that like? How did you change it?
- Is there any person, group, or thing that controls any part of your life right now? How does that feel? If you do not feel it is creative for you, what can you do to change it and allow Spirit to control?

_____
_____
_____
_____
_____
_____
_____
_____
_____
_____
_____
_____
_____
_____
_____
_____
_____
_____
_____
_____
_____
_____
_____
_____
_____
_____
_____
_____
_____

Chapter 9

How Does a Nice Jewish Boy from Brooklyn Become an African Chief?

Fasten your seat belts. (Did you ever notice that they didn't have seat belts on the Enterprise? Come on – you're travelling at light speed through space dodging meteors and Klingon photon torpedoes with no seat belts!!). We are about to traverse a time warp to move ahead about 30 years to 2006. You have probably noticed that we have left the lesser journey, my trip across America in 1975 – 76, in favor of consideration of the greater journey – The Journey of Life.

Ready for déjà vu? It's going to feel like 1975 all over again. At least it did for me. For you, it will feel like Chapter 1. Instead of 1975, it's 2006. Instead of Parsippany, NJ, it's Phoenix, Arizona. Here I am again, about to leave a great-paying career, wonderful girlfriend, good friends, and comfortable life for the great unknown. Hey – I can't help it! God's talking to me again! This time, it was in stages.

First, I became aware that it was time to quit my job. Oh, I could say it was because I was unhappy with the direction upper management was taking the company (which I was), or because they dissolved the division of which I was Director (which they did, but they allowed me to stay on in another position with the company). The truth of the matter (make that "Truth" of the matter), however, was that it was time to leave my father's house again. So I quit. No idea what I was going to do next. Just quit and waited for my next Divine instruction.

It came through AARP magazine. Moses gets a really cool burning bush, and I get AARP magazine!! Hey – who am I to tell God how to send His messages? There was an article on the Peace Corps that said 7% of all Peace Corps Volunteers are over 50. Interesting statistic, and I found it somewhat surprising since I thought ALL PCV's (try to keep up with the acronyms) were just out of college. I didn't realize what a life-changing event reading this article was to be for me.

Now, if you ask ANYBODY who knows me, they will tell you that I'm not exactly a poster boy for Peace Corps. I don't like to camp. I REALLY dislike being uncomfortable. I'm not crazy about travel outside the U.S. I don't learn languages easily. And I'm being kind to myself! I'm sure anyone else you ask will come up with several more reasons why this sudden shift in my life didn't seem to fit. So how did this happen? Well, I was no longer *unconsciously* following Divine direction like I did in 1975. I was now very aware of my own Divine Identity, and it was clear to me when I was hearing that voice. Don't get me wrong – my human capacities were not at all happy about this decision! But I had learned by this time not to let mind and heart run the ship. Just like in '75, however, I allowed them to have their security blanket. In this case, it was the knowledge that it takes about a year to process a Peace Corps application. My mind realized that the direction I had been clearly shown was to APPLY to the Peace Corps. That didn't necessarily mean that I would actually be going INTO the Peace Corps.

SPIRITUAL INSIGHT # 21: God often shows us a direction, not to get to the presumed destination, but rather just to get on the right path.

There is even a story to illustrate this point. A man who believed in Divine guidance got in his car and heard his inner voice tell him to go to 4th Street and Ridgeway Ave. As he was on his way, he heard the voice tell him to take a left on 13th Street. He objected that it was the wrong way to go, but the perception was clear to make the left so he did. Then he was told to make a right on Conant Street, another turn that would not get him to 4th and Ridgeway. He continued getting directions that took him further from his presumed destination and finally ended up at 1st Drive and Salem Avenue. He asked his inner guidance, "If you wanted me to go to 1st Drive and Salem Avenue, why didn't you tell me that to begin with?" God replied, "I knew that if you thought you were going to 1st Drive and Salem Avenue, you would never have left the house."

By this time in my life, I knew that was true. My heart and mind, therefore, took solace in thinking that I would just be starting this application process so that I would be led to the right person, place, or opportunity to continue my life in a nice, safe, and comfortable way. It would surely not include moving half way around the world to live in a village where running water and electricity would be replaced by miserable heat and insects intent on being my constant companions.

Apparently confirming this vision that I was really meant to stay in the good old US of A, a wonderful woman came into my life shortly after I had sent in my application (for the Peace Corps – not for a woman). At this point, I had given up on <u>YourPerfectPartner.com</u> or any other way of establishing a meaningful relationship, or even a pretty good weekend, since I had set course for the Peace Corps. Deciding I wanted to join a Sierra Club hike up Humphrey's Peak, Arizona's highest point, I got up at 3 am (not anything I would normally do unless under threat of death) and drove the 2 hours to Flagstaff to meet the group. Turned out to be only 5 of us but one of the other 4, Beverly (name changed to protect my hide), was something special. We laughed our way up and down the 12,633 feet (OK – I can't lie – we actually stopped at the saddle which I think is at about 11,000 feet). and I had found the connection with a woman I had longed for. Since it had happened so organically and fluidly, I knew that it had to be right.

But the internal draw towards the Peace Corps experience did not go away. As much as my heart sang when I was with Beverly, when the time came, I knew that I had to go. Reminded me of John Wayne up on his horse saying to his beloved, "A man's gotta' do what a man's gotta' do" (or was that Clint Eastwood?). It felt more painful, though, than noble when it was my life instead of a movie. Why did it happen that way? I don't know. I do know that it was not a mistake, and I do know that we had a wonderful year together. You may have heard this next insight before, but I have learned that it is absolutely true:

SPIRITUAL INSIGHT # 22: People come into our lives for a reason, a season, or a lifetime. Don't miss the value of any relationship by trying to make it something other than what it is.

And let me just say that Beverly is still very much a part of my life. We tried to hold on to the boyfriend/girlfriend relationship for a short time while I was in Africa but realized that it wasn't going to work.

We both went through some pain and came out the other side as wonderful friends.

So – I did it again. Sold or gave away just about everything I owned (which was a LOT more than in 1975!) including Shadow, my beautiful 1999 black Toyota Celica GT Convertible, and headed into the great unknown. Well, actually, I went to Philadelphia. That, however, was just for 2 days of "pre-training" where I met 47 other people (4 of which were also over 50) bound for Ghana, in West Africa. I think that 2 days is Peace Corps' way of giving everyone a last chance to say, "WHAT AM I DOING??!!" Yet, all 48 of us got on that plane and saw our next sunrise in Accra, the capital city of Ghana.

This book isn't about my Peace Corps experience (see – I told you I'd keep telling you what this book *isn't* about!), but I would like to give you a little feel for it. After all, I did mention it in the introduction; plus, I kept a journal there in the form of a blog. This IS a journaling book after all. In addition, the Peace Corps was a great experience where I learned additional spiritual insights which I would like to share with you. So pretend this is a National Geographic (without the amazing photos) and join me in Africa.

Wednesday, October 10, 2007

<u>I MADE IT!</u>

Thanks to all of you who posted comments and to those who have simply come to the site to share my experience. Some of you were probably wondering what happened to me. Not to worry – this is just the first time I could actually get to the blog site to make an entry.

Oh – before I forget – a special Hi to Carmine's Mom! She told me in Philly that you had already found my site and asked her to look up the "nice looking older man". She's doing great, as I'm sure you know, and I told her I'd say "Hi" when I got to my blog site. If you plan to send her any packages, throw in some Oreos for me! [*She DID send me Oreos!!*]

Also – congratulations to Dharma for quitting Inter-Tel and following the dream that you have already begun to materialize. You are an inspiration to many in so many ways.

What's that? Oh..... you all tuned in to find out about Ghana??!! OK – where do I start? The country is absolutely beautiful – at least the parts I've seen so far. The part of the Volta Region that I was in for a few days is lush green and looks to me like tropical rainforest although I'm told that Ghana's rainforest is in a different region. Volta has incredible mountains dressed in lush, verdant foliage with dramatic waterfalls highlighting different areas. I got to hike up to one of them and swim in a beautiful cold pool with a natural Jacuzzi built in! The cold water felt great after a pretty good hike to get up to it, although the two youngsters I went up with (Jerry's about 35 and Kim is 10 years younger than that) didn't seem to be sweating near as much as I was.

Now I'm in the Brong Ahafo Region for my 9 weeks of training. Though not as lush as what I saw in Volta, we are at the end of the rainy season and this area is plenty green and gorgeous in itself.

When we first arrived, we spent 10 days in the Accra area. Accra is the capitol of the country and is roughly the same population as Phoenix. Though I didn't find the city nearly as attractive as the other regions, people who thrive on the big city buzz can certainly find that in Accra. The thing that floored me was how incredibly nice the people were. There were 3 of us trying to find certain places in Accra as part of a Peace Corps "scavenger hunt". We stopped a man to ask him directions and he spent the next 3 hours walking us to all the places we needed to find and filling us in a lot on life in Ghana. Another man on a tro-tro (read "bus") paid the fare of all 3 of us and we hadn't even met him!!

During training, I'm staying with a family in a small village close to Techiman and this is a great way to begin to integrate into the Ghanaian culture. They have been very good to me and help me in many ways. In fact, it is very uncomfortable for me, and most Americans I think, to allow them to sweep my room, cook all my meals, and serve me, wash my clothes (and there are no washing machines – it's all done by hand in a wash tub and bucket), carry my bags, etc. etc.

Which is not to say that I'm staying at the Ritz. There are very few amenities although I am very thankful that we DO have electricity – even though there is no outlet in my room. No running water so I have learned how to take bucket baths. I've done them with cold water (and on hot nights that really does feel better) but I prefer heating up the water for my morning bath. I can get used to this for the next 2 years but I KNOW that a hot shower will be high on my list of things to do any time I get the chance! "Sleeping in" is now defined as 6:30 since the roosters start crowing around 4:15. I can't help but feel like this might be a bit of what Sharon experienced when she first moved out on her own in the Navajo reservation. We'll have to compare notes, Sharon!!

Some notes on the Ghanaians. Unlike black people in the U.S. who have diverse backgrounds and are therefore all different shades of black and brown, Ghanaians all have the same beautiful creamy, smooth skin that is somewhere between milk chocolate and dark chocolate" [*As I got to know the people, I saw that this is inaccurate. There is a range of color but not as wide a range as in the States*]. "The young men, and many of the older ones, could be in ads for LA Fitness with their 6 pack abs, broad chests and shoulders, and cut biceps and all without ever lifting a barbell or doing a push-up!! Life here is physical and rock-hard muscular bodies is a byproduct. I find many of the women to be strikingly beautiful with posture my Mom would be proud of (a direct result of carrying everything, and I mean EVERYTHING, on their heads from the time they are small girls) and a natural sensuality that is accented by their beautifully-colorful clothing. In fact, all of the clothes here are of gorgeous patterns and colors and I'm looking forward to having some made (you can get tailored clothes for under $10) but I may wait until I get to my assigned village, Daboya, in the Northern Region in December. The thing that strikes me about the children, along with how incredibly cute they are, is how little crying I hear! Oh sure – there are tears now and again but not nearly what I'm used to in the States. Even kids under 4 are remarkably well behaved and I doubt that anyone in Ghana would have any idea what "terrible twos" means!

There is so much I haven't touched on but I need to get back to my village for dinner. I'll try to get back for my next entry sometime in the next few weeks. ALL responses are welcome and feel free to ask questions.

That's it for now from your roving African reporter!!

Interesting how scared to death of the unknown most of us are. When I would tell friends and relatives that I was going to Ghana and then explained that that was in Africa (many Americans aren't the best at world geography!) so many had the same first reaction: "Is it safe there?" The visions of my imminent demise varied from jungle rot to poisonous snakes and insects to weird diseases and parasites to a spear in the back or being eaten by a tiger, which doesn't even exist in Africa! Though it's true that there are dangers in Ghana, there are also dangers in Phoenix, Des Moines, and Ft. Lauderdale; and intelligent people take appropriate precautions wherever they may be. My actual experience of Ghana, as you saw from the above post, was one of a beautiful country with diverse terrain that is fascinating to explore and of warm, friendly people very open to lending a hand to hopelessly lost and starry-eyed Westerners. If you are longing for the days when life was simple, well, check out this next blog post.

Feb 8, 2008:

It occurs to me that I've never told you all what Daboya is like. It's a relatively quiet (I'll get back to that "relatively" part in a minute) village of about 5000 adults and 4 billion children. The village has electricity but no running water. Fortunately, there is a well-developed clean water supply system in place so not a big risk here of the nasty things carried in water available from lakes, rivers, etc. Having been scared silly by the Peace Corps, however, I still boil and filter my water before drinking it.

There is almost no traffic here because the village sits on the west bank of the White Volta River...which has no bridge across it. Therefore, everything coming from the east has to get to Daboya by canoe once you get to the end of the road. It is amazing to me what they put on those canoes, but they haven't yet figured out how to get a car across (I should start a ferry service!). You can get to Daboya from the west and north by car or truck (preferably 4WD) but only in the dry season and then you better bring an extra pair of shocks! As a result, there are virtually no cars in Daboya. We have bikes, motorbikes (they DO put those on a canoe!), and a few tractors.

There is an active market in Daboya so, unlike a lot of my fellow PCV's (that's Peace Corps Volunteers for the uninitiated), I don't have to bike or hike for miles to buy any food. I can get yams, eggs, tomatos, onions, in-season fruit, and store-type items brought in from Tamale like spaghetti, tomato paste, sugar, salt, soap, toilet paper, Coke / Fanta, margarine, powdered or condensed milk, crackers, and several other items at our local market. There is also a wide (well – OK – "wide" is stretching it a bit!) variety of fish, poultry, and meat available but, being the kind of city boy who always thought that chicken just comes in shrink-wrapped, neatly cut pieces, I'm not ready to watch mine being killed and handed to me for butchering!! I'll likely be pretty close to a vegetarian for the next two years! I also go to Tamale about twice/month and there I get a wider variety of vegetables and groceries.

Daboya is 99% Muslim so it has 2 VERY small Christian churches and seemingly 1000 mosques. Now let's get back to that "relatively quiet" phrase. Since there is almost no traffic and the teens keep their "Friday night colossal record dances" down to a reasonable roar, things are quiet here........except for the 5 times/day of required Muslim prayer. Each one of those 1000 (OK, I'm exaggerating a tad) mosques has paging horns on top and it would be easy to hear the call to prayers from any one of them all over the village. Get them all going and I'm surprised my brother and sister don't hear it in Florida! It especially gets my attention at the first prayer time.... 4 am! I must admit that I'm getting used to it and didn't even wake up this morning. Maybe the power was off.............

I am more (or less?) fortunate than PCV's (remember that acronym?) in many countries because the official language of Ghana is English but don't let that fool you. There are something like 70 regional languages in Ghana. In the big cities, most people speak English but not necessarily so in the villages. Still, enough people speak English here that I can get by with my limited Gonja. I'm also fortunate because 90% of the Daboya people speak Gonja unlike many villages where you may have to become familiar with 2-3 languages, or more, to converse with the locals.

Weather here is hot and dry (like Phoenix) with "seasons" that are basically hot and **really** hot (like Phoenix) and it only rains during one time of the year (like Phoenix except that the rainy season here is 6 months instead of 6 weeks). Feb to April is the dry season when it gets nasty hot (and **unlike** Phoenix, there is no A/C here!). May to Nov is the rainy season when it cools a bit. Dec to Jan is Harmattan season when the strong winds blow cool air and tons of dust (from the Sahara Desert). So far, I have only been here during Harmattan and I love it. The locals think I am crazy because I walk around in shorts and a T-shirt. They are freezing and I get asked every day why I'm not cold. Well – I figure (no thermometers or radio weathermen here) it's about 70 degrees in the evening and maybe 50 on the coldest very early mornings. It's considerably colder than that even in Phoenix during the winter!

Well – perhaps that's enough for now. Let me know by reply to this comment if you have specific questions and I'll answer them next month. Maybe I can also give you an idea of my daily routine at that time.

Ebore Ebuganya! (That's Gonja for "May God see you safely through the night" and DON'T check the spelling!)

Going back to being scared of the unknown, we also tend to be scared of that which we don't understand and of that which we get only a limited view. Having now spent two years in a village of about 5000 Muslims, I have a firsthand experience of what kind, peaceful people they are. Yes, there are extremists in the world who are radical bullies practicing hatred and murder in the name of God, but that is no different than other religions and cultures throughout history (just read the Jewish history in the Old Testament or a history book about the Christian Crusades). What I witnessed in Daboya was a vast majority of Muslims living with a tiny minority of Christians, a percentage of those with indigenous beliefs, and 1 Jew (that would be me!) in complete peace without any religious pressure (if you don't count those paging horns!). In fact, all public events start and end with a prayer. If they start with a Muslim prayer, they end with a Christian prayer or vice versa. So next time you meet a Muslim in a grocery store, at a PTA meeting, or at a ball game, it is 100,000 times more likely that that person is a warm, peaceful person than it is that he is planning to blow up a train station. Extend your hand and your heart to him/her and you'll get the same back.

I really am only going to give you a few entries; but I figure, based on the title of this chapter, I have to include this next one.

My 4/08 Blog post:

WOW – I never even thought I would meet an African village Chief and now I are one!! My "enskinning" date was April 4, 2008 and no, it doesn't have anything to do with them removing any of my skin! It is called that because chiefs sit on animal skins when they meet. In southern Ghana, they sit on stools and it is called being enstooled. Hey – I'm not making this up!!

Anyway – I want to send my deepest appreciation and my most heart-felt apology to Cheri, Dahria, and Alicia who saw my original announcement with the date set at 3/31 and really went the extra mile (actually, a LOT more than one mile!) to come and be with me during the special day. They even brought gifts (no gold, frankincense, and myrrh though) and put up with one of the hottest days of the year. You guys are terrific and I am very glad you got to see my site but sooooo sorry that it was the wrong day. I know there were many others who would have loved to have come but it's not like jumping in the car in the States and heading cross town! I still felt your support. And Cheri was amazing....she spent her last Ghana cedi to come BACK on Thursday so she could be there for the ceremony. Seeing her there really made me feel like I was seeing not only my other PCV friends but also folks from back home so an extra special THANK YOU to Cheri. It was so nice to share that day with you.

I also have to mention the HUGE appreciation I have for my counterpart and friend Musah, even though he has no access to internet and will probably never read this. Talk about going out of your way! He not only educated me on what to expect and my responsibilities, his family did all of the cooking (I was responsible to feed what seemed like the whole village!), he opened his family compound for the celebration following the ceremony since my place is too small and too far from the Chief's Palace, he arranged for all the gifts to be delivered to the 35 or so sub-chiefs that are due gifts, he helped me shop for all of the food, he wove my smock and hat (see pics if I can figure out how to post any!), and he was an absolute rock of support even though there was a lot going on in his life at the same time. Seriously do not know how I would have done it without him.

So, what was the day like? I was at the Chief Warrior's house at 6:30 am just to receive any Chiefs that might want to greet me early. The drums called me out to start the ceremony around 9:30. The same way that you can't recall a lot of details about your own wedding, I'm not sure I remember much of the ceremony but I do have video for those who I see when I get home! I know there was drumming and ceremony including donning my new smock, hat, and walking stick and at the end, they picked me up, put me on the shoulders of a horse of a young man (who is in my English class so he daren't drop me or he'd flunk for the year!) and then carried me in the midst of a screaming throng to Musah's compound. I remember the ride clearly enough because, although I smiled all the way, I was scared to death! They don't just "carry" you, they bounce you like a trotting horse! Put that together with the uneven, unpaved ground and the milling throng and I smelled the recipe for disaster. Visions of my epitaph crossed my mind: "Here lies Larry Pearlman – killed by a fall from the shoulders of a crowd honoring him".

Of course no such fall happened, I was ceremoniously ushered into the compound and seated on a big cushion with young girls fanning me to keep me cool. I was VERY happy to have Cheri close by to talk to as my Gonja still does not lend itself to prolonged conversations! I sat there most of the afternoon as people came by to greet me, eat, and generally enjoy themselves. Late in the afternoon, the drummers came back and the girls from Musah's school did the Tora dance for me. What a kick! Kind of a cross between the Bump (if you remember that, then you're well over 40!) and Bumper Cars. Great fun to watch but I'm betting that several of those girls needed ice packs on their hips that night!

So now I am known as QuartersWura, which means Chief of the Quarters, referring to the hostel in which I live and the Teacher's Quarters that are in the same area. Anything that relates to those places comes under my "jurisdiction" so I'm hoping no conflicts come up in the next 2 years!! I also have to wear my hat and carry my walking stick everywhere I go or I can be fined by the Paramount Chief! And EVERYWHERE I go, people greet me with shouts of "Garba" which means Chief. I'm sure the novelty will wear off after a while but it's fun now.

Speaking of that, it IS fun but I also realize that it is a huge honor and I appreciate that. My Peace Corps supervisor, who has been in Africa for 5 years, told me that he has never heard of any Peace Corps Volunteer being enskinned (or enstooled) in such a short time so it is a responsibility and privilege that I take seriously.

Well – that's the big news from my end of the pond for now. I'll be in touch again soon.

Love you All ....QuartersWura

Would this make a GREAT MasterCard commercial or what??!!

Chief's walking stick - $15

Smock and Hat - $50

Feeding the Village - $200

Becoming an African Chief – Priceless

Actually, I DID present this to MasterCard but I ran into enough red tape that I just dropped the whole idea.

Here are some thoughts after being in my village for about a year:

November, 2008

Impressions of Northern Ghana

A young girl running next to a bus in 100-degree heat to make sure someone gets their 15 pesewa (15 cents) change for the Pure Water sachet they bought through the window when the bus stopped at a traffic light.

A farmer with a dusty, torn open shirt coming down the dirt path from his farm after sundown – his broad chest glistening black with sweat, his ever present cutlass (machete) bound to the burlap bag of maize on the back of his bicycle with a rubber inner tube, and his bright, white teeth in a broad grin as he greets me.

Three market women pounding fufu together in a perfectly syncopated rhythm.

Children walking to school in their uniforms – blue for the Jr. Secondary School, brown for the primary school, and kind of Gingham for the pre-school.

Strong, graceful women walking back into town from the bush with a pile of firewood balanced seemingly effortlessly on their heads.

A baby suckling his mother's breast on a crowded bus while the stranger beside her holds her other baby.

A cargo truck filled so impossibly with people hanging off every side that you just know it will topple over when it hits one of the innumerable deep ruts in what is supposed to be a road. Sometimes, it does.

Fishermen sitting and patiently repairing their nets like a seamstress sewing a dress.

Incredibly beautiful and varied cloud formations morphing into brilliant textured canvas for the evening's sunset.

An outside wall bathed in fluorescent light so thickly covered with flying insects that you cannot tell what color the wall is.

Baby goats cavorting with each other just the day after they were born.

The Muslim call to prayer issuing from a dozen mosques' speakers at 4 am, 1 pm, 3 pm, 6 pm, and again at 7:30 pm.

Men napping under trees during the heat of the day.

Students standing and saying, in unison, "Good Morning Sir. How are you Sir?" when their teacher walks into the classroom.

Women in their brightly colored two-yards resembling a garden of beautiful flowers.

A gathering of chiefs in their traditional smocks and hats sitting at the feet of the Paramount Chief, heatedly discussing the case before them in their native tongue.

Magical Kapok and majestic Dawadawa trees.

Celebrations – weddings, passing outs (graduations), naming ceremonies, enskinments, festivals – happening at the Bode (town square) or at someone's family compound. And the seemingly daily funerals.

Ebunto (the riverside) – busy with women doing wash, women carrying water in huge basins on their heads, beggars, canoes with travelers, tourists, bicycles and motos, goats, sheep, and cattle, huge bags of maize, cassava, and groundnuts headed for the Tamale market, smaller canoes with fishermen, and people bathing or cooling off in the river.

The barrenness of the dry season being engulfed by the jungle-like greenery of the rainy season.

Children running barefoot moving a large wheel rim next to them with a stick – bringing to mind the time in America of Tom Sawyer and Huck Finn.

People sleeping on the ground outside of their rooms because it is too hot to sleep inside.

The sky turned brown with the desert sand and high winds of the Harmattan (Dec / Jan)

½ built homes everywhere.

Beautiful night skies.

Chop bar "fast food".

Infants sleeping in impossible heat wrapped to their mother's back in a two-yard.

Barefoot girls of all ages playing / dancing Ampe.

Futbol (soccer) matches on dusty fields.

A small boy with doe's eyes leading a blind woman beggar to cars at a traffic light.

These are just some of the images that will be with me the rest of my life connecting me to Ghana. I cannot do them justice with these few words but I hope they bring you some feel of what my world is like.

I'll bet by now you are wondering if I ever did any actual *work* during my time in the Peace Corps. Well, since you asked………

June, 2009

This has been a productive month. Our permanent Visitors' Centre has moved to the next level. All construction materials are on site and boy was it interesting watching 30 or so young men from the local youth group transport 100 bags of cement, 50 plywood sheets, 74 long iron rods, a large Polytank (to handle the water for our flush toilets (YAY!!), many 5 gallon buckets of paint, about 10 boxes of nails, about 70 metal roofing sheets, a bunch of lumber, and assorted other materials to the site. All of that had to be unloaded from the cargo truck on the other bank of the river, then loaded on to canoes (many trips!) to cross the river, then loaded on to a hand truck, tractor (2 loads), and heads, shoulders, and backs to get it up the hill to the site, then unloaded, and finally moved into our temporary office where it will be stored. Ladies, you would have enjoyed seeing all of these rippling muscles glistening with sweat as these young men went about the task easily and with joy – even though we didn't finish until 9:00 at night. Tractor loads of smooth river sand and rough sand were brought to the site and a crew molded the cement blocks needed to do the job. The trained construction crew from Nature Conservation Resource Centre (NCRC) – the NGO [*non-governmental organization*] who is providing this building – will be back in July to finish the construction and then it will be time to CELEBRATE!! It promises to be the nicest building in Daboya.

And FINALLY our area sanitation meetings are happening. It took me a year to figure out that when it comes to something like this it is better to work through the elders of each of the 16 areas of Daboya than try to coordinate the entire village. It also took a long time (Hey – I'm a little slow, OK??!!) to figure out that it is better to have area meetings at night (8pm). Farmers are all back from farm, fishermen from fishing, weavers have packed up their looms, women have finished all chores, and people actually come to the meetings! So we have now had meetings in just about all the areas and the response has been very good. Now we just have to hope for consistent follow through and we will have a cleaner, healthier, and more beautiful Daboya!

Ghana Tourist Board is helping us put together a preliminary brochure and a lot of the same information will be useful for websites. I have provided the information to 3 different organizations for inclusion on websites they are working on.

A Guest House (hotel – sort of) has been built by a private citizen and is just about ready for use. It has a FLUSH TOILET AND REAL SHOWER!!! In the future, he will be adding a kitchen and bar as well as a store to sell the smocks, hats, dresses, and other items that are woven here. I'm hoping that he has the facility open for business by the end of July and then you can all come and visit!

AND one of the Peace Corps Volunteers in my group got married this month as well. His wife is a wonderful, beautiful Ghanaian woman and it was a kick to attend the wedding. For those who are wondering if we danced semi-naked around a huge campfire to the sound of rhythmic jungle drums, I have to disappoint you and tell you that they were married in a Pentecostal church! Nevertheless, it was interesting to see the cultural differences that show up in small ways in the wedding ceremony and at the reception. Since there were 12 Peace Corps Volunteers among the 100 or so guests, it was also a very nice reunion for us. The wedding was in the southern part of the country so I hadn't seen any of these folks for quite some time. It was worth the 7 hour round-trip bus / tro-tro ride that I endured as part of a day that started at 4:45 am and got me back to Tamale at 8 pm.

Now we look forward to July and all that will fill it.

And finally, my thoughts toward the end of my time in Daboya (I left there in early November, 2009):

August, 2009

A cold bucket bath – bargaining with a taxi driver – pit latrines – walking 200 yards to GET to the pit latrine – eating Fufu with Okra stew with my fingers out of a communal bowl with 3 other people – seeing women carrying heavy loads of firewood, water, goods for sale, and so many other things on their head – going weeks without seeing another white person – seeing the most beautiful colors in what was unfamiliar clothing – actually seeing the Milky Way clearly along with a zillion stars – knowing that EVERY day will be 100 degrees and there is no A/C – watching baby goats play in the most joyful way – being greeted by just about EVERYBODY when you walk down the street – never hearing an airplane, helicopter, or train – living without DVD's, TV, movies, bowling, golf, or fast food – walking in a stately procession with 20 Chiefs enroute to the weekly Chiefs' meeting.

These are just a few of Life's events that started out 2 years ago as "experiences", as in, "Now THAT was an experience!" Then all those individual experiences began to blend into a grand adventure. Before I knew it, that adventure had become simply my life. Now, and I say this with some sadness, it has all become part of the routine of my day. Which is not to say that I don't still appreciate the joy and the beauty that I see around me OR that I don't mutter under my breath at times about the uncomfortable things, but it's no longer the same as it was when I first experienced these things.

Think of it as dating. Remember the glorious excitement and wonderful discoveries at the beginning? You may still love the person after 5 years or 50 years. In fact, the love may be much deeper and more significant than it ever was when you were in the early days. But the feeling can never be the same in the sense of the discovery of newness. What was once strange and/or exotic or simply unknown and is now known cannot become unknown again, no matter how wonderful (or awful) it may be.

This is what truly sets Peace Corps apart from most, if not all, of the other organizations working to help developing countries. You can't understand a culture during a two week vacation or even a 3-6 month working assignment. And you don't get to really "grok" (check out Robert Heinlein's "Stranger in a Strange Land" if you don't know that word. It's a good read) the pulse of a village by living in a condo in the big city and visiting the site in an air conditioned SUV 1-2 days/week. This is not to suggest that NGO's and other governmental organizations aren't doing good things. Obviously they are and Peace Corps relies heavily on good working relationships with many of them. After all, Peace Corps brings no money to the table, although it takes over a year living in the village to convince them that you're not rich and do not have the means to fund a library, high school, futbol (read "soccer") field, and bowling alley (OK – nobody in Daboya has asked me for a bowling alley but it sounds like a neat idea). So how do we make a difference? By blending into the community and discovering from the inside what they REALLY need and want and will support. Then, a PC Volunteer (PCV) can go to work and find ways, many include NGO's and government organizations, to fund these projects, help to supervise both the external parties and the village people involved, and train local personnel in everything from tree planting to annual reports so that the project becomes sustainable long after the foreign faces and accents are gone from the community.

A tourist gets the "experience". A 3-6 month NGO volunteer gets the adventure. But only people like missionaries, those who move to a country to live there, and PCV's get to make a new culture part of their lives and established routines. I've had my ups and downs here (and thanks to all of you who have supported me in SO many ways to ease the way through those "downs") but I am very glad that I got to move through the whole cycle to come beyond "me and those interesting people" to simply "us" and having "my living quarters" morph into "my home".

And, when all goes well, there might, or might not, be something tangible to show for our efforts. In the case of our tourism efforts in Daboya, we actually now have a building (thanks primarily to Nature Conservation Resource Center and funding from the European Union). So feast your eyes (if I can get the photo to download properly) on Daboya's new Visitors' Centre!! We still have some landscaping to do and the signage isn't up yet but we are open for business so ya'll come!! We can share a bowl of banku with groundnut stew or, if you're a wussy, I'll make you a fruit salad and tuna sandwich!

I learned a lot of lessons during those 27 months in Ghana. I learned that, in America, we grossly underestimate and over-protect our children. I learned that a society or an individual doesn't have to be driven by the clock and that a relationship-based society has some beautiful advantages over a time-based society (although there are benefits to both). I learned that circumstances may vary widely but people are people and no matter where we are in the world, we laugh, cry, bleed, love one another, irritate one another, yearn, die, grieve, play and work and it's really not all that different. I learned that we are WAY too sensitive and politically correct in America. There is so much more that I learned in that short time but maybe the most important thing was:

SPIRITUAL INSIGHT # 23: The richest person is not the one who has the most but the one who needs the least.

That rolls off the tongue rather easily and may sound comfortably spiritual but a friend asked me if I really thought that a monk was richer than Bill Gates. Well – I really don't know Bill Gates and it would very much depend on which monk you were considering. The whole point here is that the richness of your life experience has NOTHING to do with how much money you have. Bill Gates may indeed be a VERY rich man in terms of how fulfilled he is in the life he leads. A monk without a dollar to his name may be just as rich in that sense as Bill Gates. In neither case is the richness of that person's life – or yours - measured by a financial statement. And the matter of need is not limited to material assets.

When I was in Daboya, I had very little in terms of "stuff" and I was quite satisfied with, and thankful for, what I did have. But when emotional needs arose, like when I was sick and longed for someone to pamper me a bit, or mental needs, like when I wanted to be able to carry on a conversation deeper than my piddling grasp of Gonja would allow, then my experience of the fullness of Life was less and I felt poorer for it. On the days when my circumstances were the same but I accepted them and didn't feel a ***need*** for those things, I was a richer man.

Pretty simple really. If I feel like I need something than, by definition I am feeling a lack. When I feel no lack, I am a rich person. Want an example? Visit Daboya and watch a 10 year old boy thrilled with life as he kicks around a clod of dirt, pretending it is a soccer ball (he'll call it a futbol). Compare that to a 10 year old boy from a wealthy family in the U.S. moping because his parents won't let him have the latest X-Box. Who has the richer experience?

Maybe that's a good lead-in question to bring us to the chapter you have all been waiting for – the one where we finally answer the question of questions, "Who am I REALLY?"

Possible Questions to Consider in Your Journal

- Have you ever been led by inner guidance to go in a direction only to end up somewhere other than where you thought you were going? Would you have started on the journey if you knew that was your final destination? Write about it and see if there is more to learn.

- Who is someone that was in your life for a "reason"? What was the reason? What lessons did you take from the relationship? When someone was in your life for a "season", were you able to accept the fact that it was time for them to leave? Describe your feelings around it and reflect on the value of that season. Who do you just know is going to be part of your entire lifetime? What are the things that connect and bind you? Write them a letter telling them what they mean to you.

- You don't have to go to Africa to experience a culture foreign to you. There are "mini-cultures" all around us. It might be someone else's religion, race, political party, or occupation. It might be quilters, horse people, square-dancers, or hikers. It could simply be the Mars / Venus dichotomy of the sexes. Choose some "culture" that is somehow unfamiliar to you and journal on the lessons you can learn from that culture. You might want to first sit with a person who is in that culture and simply ask them questions with the intent of listening and learning.

- Other than food, water, air, and basic shelter, what are the things that you think you "need"? Make a list of 10. Consider each one separately. If you don't have it, how do you feel about that? If you do have it and lost it, how do you think you would feel? Do you know anyone who doesn't have it and who doesn't feel deprived? Why do you think these things are so important to you? What would need to change in you for you to feel fulfilled without these things?

Chapter 10

So Who Am I REALLY?

Remember back in Chapter 3 when I said that my intended destination was San Jose? It was not San Jose. That was just a smoke screen to keep my conscious mind comfortable thinking it had some semblance of control over this journey. It was not Phoenix, even though that was where I settled in for 32 years. It was not Loveland, Colorado, even though that is where I currently reside. In fact, it wasn't any place on

Earth. My real destination, unbeknownst (isn't that a great word?!!) to my conscious mind was a new consciousness. As mentioned in that same chapter, I didn't even **have** to leave NJ to get there. It was, however, a lot more adventurous this way and it sure opened me up to a whole lot of interesting people, places, and experiences that I might not have had otherwise.

Now that I have written enough chapters to justify this book, I can give you the answer to the question that, through the ages, has haunted philosophers, religious people, scientists, and cute little girls with red pigtails and freckles: WHO AM I REALLY?

Here are a couple of hints:

December 15, 1976 – Wednesday – 9:30 AM

Something flashed on me last night. My position as compared to 15 months ago looks pretty bad on paper. My job (and career) is gone, my group of friends are gone, my girl is gone, my hobbies (bowling / Corvette club) are gone, and now even my car is gone. Yet I, in no way, feel defeated or deprived or down on my situation. I haven't lost anything because I carry Life wherever I go. That is why I can build another life so easily every time I move. When you carry Life with you, you can never lose it or leave it behind.

January 29, 1977 – Saturday 3:00 PM

Truth has shown itself through experience once again. While stuck out here at the airport again, I've been watching some of the other drivers. What I saw was what is meant by "you are constant regardless of your circumstance." I've been a student, a sales engineer, a salesman, a hotel worker, a factory worker, a cab driver and probably a hundred other labels but what I am doesn't change. I may be driving a cab now, but I certainly don't fit the stereotype of cab driver any more than I did GE Sales Engineer.

I also gave you a hint back in Chapter 5 when I said that your identity is the Love that you express while you do that which brings you your greatest fulfillment. It has been said that God is Love. There is your answer:

SPIRITUAL INSIGHT # 24: Your true identity is God

WAIT – Don't throw the book away and call me crazy. Hey – you've read almost 10 chapters already. Give me another paragraph or two; THEN, if you still want to, throw the book away and call me crazy.

I'm not saying that "you" – the human flesh body that has been trying to lose that annoying 10 pounds for years now – are the omnipotent, omniscient, all-powerful creator of the Universe. I am saying, though, that that entity has manifested on Earth through the faculties of body, mind, and heart that you have thought yourself to be (Not ALL of God, but what could be described as a God-Being.) You have always thought of yourself as a **Human**-Being. If you have had any experience of God in your life, then you probably thought of yourself as a human-being having a spiritual experience. As long as your consciousness remains in that place – the place of identifying with the physical, mental, and emotional capacities – that statement is true. That is exactly what is happening. On the other hand, the moment, and it only takes a moment, that you become conscious of the **God**-Being infilling those capacities, you can choose to identify with that and realize that **THAT** is the truth of whom you are. In that moment comes the recognition that you are truly a Spiritual Being – a Divine Being - having a human experience here on Earth. Way back on the first page of Chapter 1, a journal entry from 11/6/75 referenced my belief that I was 48% my emotions and 52% my mind. In human consciousness that may have been true; but in God consciousness I am ENTIRELY Divine Spirit being expressed *through* mind and emotions. Instead of feeling Love pouring forth through "you", you know that you ARE the Love, and YOU are pouring forth through the earthly capacities with which you have been blessed.

In chapter 7, I promised to tell you how to have the best sex of your life. Well, this is the secret. When a man and a woman each fully recognizes that she/he is, in fact, the Divine Feminine/Divine Masculine in expression on earth, and they join together intimately, they have the experience of literally "making love". This is not an experience that is simply between the two of them. It is a radiant, powerful blessing that moves out and has an impact on both of their worlds.

This power is not limited to the relationship between a man and a woman. The recognition, acceptance, and full expression of Divine Identity is the whole point of the journey. It is not the "end" of the journey. The journey never ends. It is eternal, and it is glorious. You don't have to die to be in Heaven.

SPIRITUAL INSIGHT # 25: Heaven is right here, right now, when you accept your true identity.

Possible Questions to Consider in Your Journal

- Write down some observations you have about your body, your mind, and your emotional realm. Who is doing the observing? Have you ever had what you considered a spiritual experience? What was it like? What were the qualities of Life that you felt moving through your body, mind, and emotions during that experience? Do you feel any identification with those qualities?
- Describe a time in your life when you have created or experienced "Heaven" regardless of the external circumstances. Describe a time when you have created or experienced "hell" when those around you appeared to be happy.
- What does "God" mean to you? In what ways do you think that God finds expression on Earth? Write about any experience you have had that you think might have been God being manifested on Earth. If you don't think you have had such an experience, how do you think it might look and feel? If you can't imagine it, think of God expressing through someone you know or have heard about (Moses, Jesus, Gandhi, Mother Teresa, your priest, rabbi, or Imam) and identify the qualities appearing through that person that you consider Godly. What opportunities do you have in your life to express those same qualities?

Epilogue

I gave the first draft of my book to my friend Phyllis to read and give me feedback. She told me that I left out the pain in my life and that readers would want to know about that part of me. She also pointed out that I hadn't even mentioned my 20 year marriage and my son. I countered that that is not what this book is about (sound familiar??). But she got me when she said that the readers (that would be you) might discount all of my lofty spiritual insights based on an impression that I had had such an easy life that it was pretty easy to spout off spiritual platitudes since I never had to test them under fire. OK Phyl – you win. God, I hate it when you're right!!

But this is not an autobiography and not the place for detailed scrutiny of that portion of my life. Perhaps a brief view of a specific event will give a fuller picture of who I am and what challenges I have had to test out my spiritual mettle. Although I am excerpting here the portion of this part of my life representing my greatest pain, it should be noted that my years with my wife and son were filled with a great deal of joy and love.

Mary Bane was the piano player for the Phoenix Emissary choir and our choir director, Carol Amey, convinced me that I could sing well enough to be in the choir – as long as I stood between two men also singing my part! Mary played like an Angel. She also had great intuitive perception, was a gourmet cook, fabulous hostess, and had a HUGE heart, zest for life and a wild mane of red hair that would draw out the beast in any man. We were moving down the same spiritual path together with The Emissaries and we married in 1980. Part of the package was a beautiful, tow-headed 10 year old (he was 7 when we started dating) boy named Brandon. Brandon grew into a 6' 6" Adonis that all mothers want for their daughters. He was kind beyond measure, polite, respectful, very smart, athletically gifted, loved poetry, history, literature, and excelled at anything he found interesting. Six months after I taught him chess, I didn't stand a chance without cheating (which of course I would NEVER do!).

But things don't always go according to a fairy tale script. Mary lost 3 pregnancies while we were married. Brandon's body stopped producing serotonin and, by the time we figured out what was going on, he was deeply, clinically depressed. In 1999, 7 months shy of his 29th birthday, Brandon drove his pick-up truck into the Arizona desert, set it on fire, and pulled the trigger of a sawed off shotgun with the barrel in his mouth.

Losing a child – especially an only child and especially to suicide – is one of the hardest things that a person ever has to face. Though we had known this could happen, it was still devastating at a personal level. For me, it was understanding – no, more than understanding; it was truly KNOWING – the spiritual principles of Life that brought me through this experience. As a God Being expressing myself on Earth through human facilities, I know that Life does not – CANNOT – die. The beautiful Being that I was blessed to know as Brandon for 21 years, the Being that I knew as son and who knew me as Dad, was gone in terms of that form but that unconquerable Spirit of Love will never die. As his father, I would have given anything to help him come past the depression and experience the full release of that Spirit while he was in form on Earth. Brandon could not accept that possibility. Still, that incredible Angel trying to find presence on this planet WAS released when Brandon chose to end the life of his human form. I know that Angel well and I know that he wasn't lost in that burning truck. There are still times when his Spirit is with me. I kept a jacket and a shirt of his and I still wear them, not in some maudlin attempt to keep him close to me, but rather as a celebration in form of that magnificent Spirit.

Mary moved out of the house as she couldn't bear to live there. We did not continue on the same path, although we shared the same spiritual principles. I continued to support her financially but we grieved in very different ways, me talking to everyone and her going into solitude, and continued to drift apart, eventually divorcing. I know the Angel that is known as Mary and, even fighting her own depression at the loss of her son and marriage, her radiance is still seeking ways to come through her and bless her world.

So my life was not simply a bowl of cherries and neither is yours. But even that has its upside. If we were never challenged then we might never be drawn to look deep inside and discover who we truly are. Here is a quote from a wise man and a good friend, Chris Foster:

"In recent years, I have come to see that what I was seeking all my life – something that is difficult to describe, but which can be experienced – is a deeper connection with my own unconquerable spirit. A deeper awareness of the stillness and peace of my own being as the winds of change roar…The pain, trauma and tribulations I have known in life – and there have been plenty – are insignificant compared to this stillness that I love. It is my own stillness. Feelings of anxiety and distress still arise – but always this stillness is present."

Countless times I have heard sweet, kind people empathize with me and conjecture on how hard it must be to lose a child. If I was nothing more than a human being having occasional spiritual experiences, then it might have been too much to bear. But as a Spiritual Being inhabiting a human body, I recognized the tragedy of an amazing Angel with extraordinary capacities of body, mind, and heart trapped by depression and low self-esteem. Brandon's gifts, even under those circumstances, touched all who met him. They couldn't help but notice his gentle spirit, kindness, intelligence, and a smile that gave a hint of the radiant, divine energy awaiting full release. When I am in the stillness that Chris talks about, I know the joy of celebrating the full release of that divine energy.

As has been said, "Pain is inevitable in every life. Suffering is optional." The spiritual insights presented in this book have been proven out time and again throughout history. Some who have lived them, you have heard of: Abraham, Joseph, Noah, Moses, Jesus, Gandhi, Mother Theresa, and others. Many have walked this earth in anonymity and yet also lived these truths. I have been privileged to know some of those people and have mentioned them in this book. The reason I can speak personally of these insights with conviction is that I have proved them out on my journey. I invite you to do the same.